W9-BWY-662

# MAKEOVER

## HOW MOBILE FLIPPED THE SHOPPING CART
(AND WHAT TO DO ABOUT IT!)

**STEPHAN SCHAMBACH**

FOREWORD BY SCOTT GALLOWAY, FOUNDER AND CHAIRMAN, L2

**NEWSTORE**
BOSTON, MA

Published by
NewStore, Inc.
Boston, MA

Publisher's Cataloging-in-Publication Data
Schambach, Stephan.

Makeover : how mobile flipped the shopping cart (and what to do about it!) / Stephan Schambach. – Boston, MA : NewStore, Inc., 2017.

p. ; cm.

ISBN13: 978-0-9980150-0-2

1. Mobile commerce. 2. Electronic commerce. I. Title.

HF5548.34.S33 2017

658.872 – dc23 2017902898

FIRST EDITION

Project coordination by Jenkins Group, Inc.
www.BookPublishing.com

Interior design by Brooke Camfield

Interior graphics design by Daniel Brylla

Printed in the United States of America

21 20 19 18 17 • 5 4 3 2 1

# Contents

# Foreword

*by Scott Galloway, Founder and Chairman, L2*

There's no better person to write a book about retail's technology transformation than someone who lived and led it. Since 1992, Stephan Schambach has founded and presided over several companies built on the premise that the next wave of technology was about to disrupt retail.

He created the world's first ecommerce software company, Intershop, which generated €123 million in annual revenue in 2000 and became a multi-billion-dollar market cap company. In 2004, Stephan recognized that all direct-to-consumer companies would need tools to update their web and mobile presence more often and faster than traditional in-house systems allowed. He moved to Boston to build Demandware, which invented the first cloud-based ecommerce platform and continues to offer the industry's leading online merchandising tools and software. Its 300+ client list, which includes digital leaders L'Oréal, Barneys, Hugo Boss, Panasonic, and Columbia Sportswear, is a testament to how much Stephan has transformed retail in the past 10 years. Demandware went public on the New York Stock Exchange (DWRE) in March 2012 and sold to Salesforce for $2.8 billion – more than six times its IPO valuation – in Q2 2016.

Unlike the cloud in 2004 and ecommerce in 1995, mobile is not the future. Mobile has already arrived. As of 2015, consumers were spending two-thirds of their digital time on mobile devices. This time is rapidly increasing while desktop usage is flat and beginning to decline. The mobile-first life extends to commerce. Mobile commerce is expected to grow at double-digit rates every year in the coming years, and 60% of shoppers now say they shop and buy on their smartphones.

While consumers are already living mobile-first lives, brands are struggling to adapt outdated desktop practices to the mobile screen. At L2 Inc., the research and consulting firm I founded, we have repeatedly named the siloed ecommerce divisions as the barrier to full and effective digital overhauls of organizations. The biggest mistake retailers make is measuring the return on their digital investments based on their ecommerce sales rather than on overall sales. While ecommerce sales make up less than 10% of overall retail sales, digitally influenced sales are estimated to be more than $1.7 trillion. Furthermore, consumers who interact with a retailer online convert at a 20% higher rate.

This new set of consumer demands could spell the end of brands that are oblivious to the new order, since 85% of shoppers will not give a brand a second chance after a poor user experience. This highlights how important it is for retailers to be informed and ready to adapt to these new patterns.

Becoming a mobile-first business does not end with hiring and using new services. Brands and retailers should approach every decision and new feature from the point of view of the mobile-obsessed consumer, which is why I highly recommend *Makeover*. It is one of the best books written on the disruption of retail.

*Introduction:*

# Why I Write This Book

We live in the age of flipped expectations.

Every day, it seems, someone upends the world in order to offer something new and better.

How can businesses stay ahead? There's a clue in the turmoil.

Ridesharing services took advantage of new technology to create businesses built around dynamically matching drivers with customers anytime, anywhere. The popularity of the personalized ride reveals a key truth about success in any industry today. For those businesses worried about disruption and those newcomers wondering how to break through and thrive, companies like Uber and Lyft delivered the secret. The secret is mobile.

Mobile technology is the building block of the next age of success. Businesses that embrace mobile will thrive. Businesses that reject it will stumble. This has been decreed not by consultants or analysts but by consumers. Armed with the power of a screen that is always and literally in hand, customers have shrugged off location shackles. Mobile beckons businesses to follow or die.

Today's consumers live in a completely mobile society. The centerpiece of their existence is no longer their street address but their smartphone. It travels with them, nests in their pockets, sits on their desks, and rests by their bedside. It's everywhere the consumer is – at home, at work, at the coffee shop, and at all stops in between. The phone isn't just by our sides; it's who we are. A misplaced smartphone, for many, is a genuine emergency.

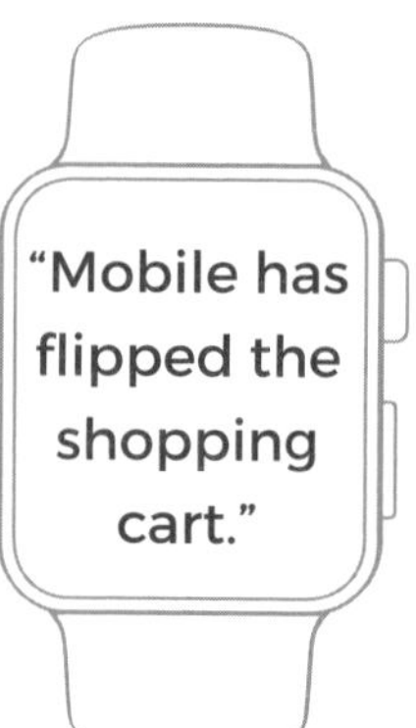


Because customers are mobile and the screen is mobile, services must also be mobile in order to fit into this new, ever-moving landscape. As the ridesharers taught us all, consumers are on the move and so are their screens. Businesses have no choice but to keep up.

This is not news to retailers. Companies with physical locations or desktop-friendly websites have seen their customers' eyes wander to the small screen. They see them in the stores, carrying phones as they shop. They observe customers averting their eyes from in-store displays and signage and even from live salespeople to look for information and entertainment. Ecommerce has seen this, too, in the abandoned web-based shopping carts and cumbersome registration pages newly mobile customers decline to embrace. What was once cutting-edge is now too hard to manage on the small screen. The new technology has changed customer expectations. Mobile has flipped the shopping cart.

Customers have fundamentally changed. Retail must transform, too, for the mobile age. That's why I wrote this book.

I meet retailers every day who tell me they're experiencing mobile's impact. They see the disruptive shockwaves rippling through the retail industry. They want to integrate mobile into their businesses. But how?

This is not the first time I've been part of disruption in my career. I was part of the first wave of ecommerce, creating Intershop, the first standard software for online shopping, in 1992. Later I founded Demandware, a software technology company providing a cloud-based ecommerce platform for retailers and brand manufacturers around the world. I then saw that the next step in serving customers will be the move to mobile.

The answer is not simple. According to our original research, NewStore's 2016 *Mobile Retail Report*, only 45% of the 112 retailers audited had an app[1]. Of those, only half were shoppable apps. What's more, none of the retailers' native apps learned consumer preferences to show more relevant products.

Still, a mobile makeover is possible with planning, perseverance, and partnership. This makeover requires far more than purchasing new technology. As customers have been transformed by mobile, retailers must follow suit. This isn't a new bell or whistle. It's a makeover, head to toe, to match mobile consumers' now always-on mobile experiences. Mobile customers, with their thumbs on their Instagram apps and the world in the palms of their hands, demand nothing less.

The good news is that mobile transformation is already starting. Old-line department stores are going mobile. So are web-based ecommerce sites and luxury brands. For forward-thinking retailers, the transformation is underway. As a result, the road map for the rest of the industry is taking shape.

In this book, we'll walk through the elements needed to thrive in a mobile world and make the argument that this world demands much more than a "tweak" in technology. It requires a transformation of the entire organization to encompass people, processes, and culture. Every aspect of the business, every relationship a retailer has, must be re-examined, reconfigured, and reintroduced. Retail must transform for the mobile age. This will mean much more than shifting channels or upgrading software. Retailers must look at all their relationships and reassess, reconfigure, and relaunch. This will not be simple, but it's necessary, and it's within reach for the retailer or brand with the motivation to make it happen.

The challenge is great and the stakes are high, but the path forward is visible, right there, in the palm of your customer's hand.

Stephan Schambach

## *Chapter 1*

# The Customer Relationship Makeover

**Insights**

- Humanity has already flipped to mobile. It's on retail to keep up.
- Mobile transforms and enhances the retailer/customer relationship.

*It's not you; it's me.*

This is a red flag in any relationship, and retailers are hearing it a lot lately in the form of customers leaving department stores, malls, and even early ecommerce companies for the mobile screen.

The numbers show the trend. Mobile commerce is expected to grow from $123 billion in 2016 to $242 billion in 2020[2]. Already, people spend more time on mobile apps than they do watching TV. Just over 70% of all shoppers surveyed in 2016 reported using digital services before their trip;

55% of millennials and 44% of non-millennials used digital services during the shopping trip[3]. The data is clear: mobile has arrived.

The advent of mobile has struck hard at the core of successful retail – the customer relationship. Brands that once boasted strong ties to their customer base now see those ties tested. Relationships that once seemed unshakable are fraying. And new companies entering the marketplace now find the rules for establishing and maintaining customer relationships are rapidly shifting and evolving, leaving little room for error.

Over

**70%**

**of shoppers used digital services before shopping in a retail store.**

Source: The Digital Divide, Deloitte, 2016

**By 2020, Mobile Commerce Will Grow 97%!**

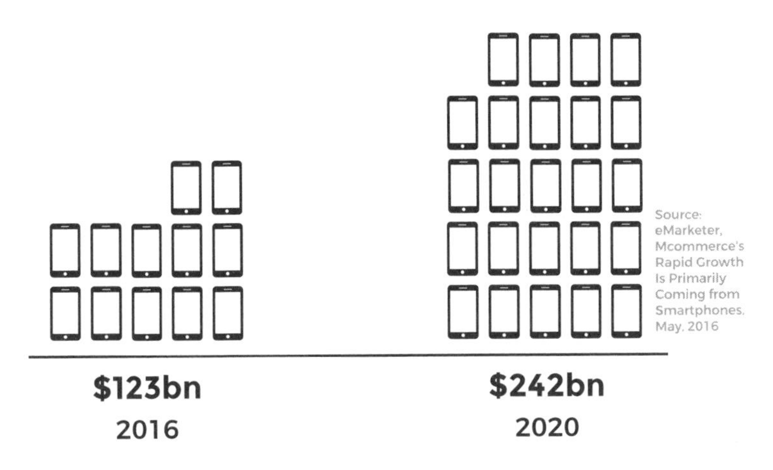


Shoppers freely acknowledge they're leaving their long-time retail outlets because mobile beckons. They recognize they're the ones driving the split, since mobile has opened their eyes to alternative possibilities. While they were once satisfied with the state of retail, the new experiences of the mobile world have reconfigured their standards. What was once acceptable is now under scrutiny. The shopping experiences that were formerly the norm have now been flipped and are being reevaluated by millions of shoppers, millions of times, every day.

Who can blame them? Let's look at two possible shopping scenarios.

Meet Jane. Jane begins her day by commuting to work on the train. One morning, she uses her phone to browse an app from her favorite boutique retailer. She downloaded the app, which came with a 10% discount on her next purchase, after a recent visit to the store. Now she's looking for a pair of shoes to wear to an upcoming event. A push notification from the app alerts her to sales, which she browses during her ride. Later that day, while waiting in line at a coffee shop, she browses the app again.

After work, she reviews items she's flagged as "favorites" on the app and narrows her choices to two pairs. Despite placing both pairs of shoes in the app's shopping basket, Jane opts not to complete the purchase through her phone because she wants to see the exact color of the shoes and try them on.

The next day, Jane drops by the boutique after work. After detecting a beacon signal, the store app notifies a sales associate about Jane's arrival. The sales associate quickly scans the store app and identifies the shoes that hold Jane's interest. This allows the two of them to engage in a relevant conversation and enjoy instant rapport.

Jane mentions her upcoming weekend event. She points out that the shoes match a dress she purchased two months earlier at the boutique's other store across town. The sales associate knows exactly which dress Jane is referring to since the smartphone depicts it as part of her purchase history.

In the store, Jane tries on one of the pairs of shoes she researched the day before. The size she thought would work feels too tight. The associate checks inventory on the spot using the store app and tells Jane they can ship the shoes in the slightly bigger size from another store directly to her home. In the meantime, she can try on the style that is very similar to check the fit.

Jane confirms that the slightly bigger size fits well. She uses Apple Pay to make the purchase. Jane receives her shoes later that evening at her home.

Now, meet Steve. Steve has several important client meetings coming up, and he wants to look sharp. At lunch, Steve decides to make a quick trip to his favorite high-end store.

He picks out several items. One shirt is not available in his size, so he approaches a sales associate, who offers to have it shipped from another store. Another shirt he's chosen needs alterations, so Steve arranges to have that delivered to his office when it's ready.

Steve is pleased – until he follows the sales associate to the cash register. The associate must use a desktop monitor and the process is laborious. The associate, looking at one desktop monitor, must log in to four different systems in order to complete Steve's order. Only one of those systems can read the magnetic swipe of his credit card. For the other three systems, the sales associate must type in the credit card number manually. The checkout process takes nearly 15 minutes, during which time Steve spies other customers approaching the register, waiting a few minutes, observing the burdensome work of Steve's checkout process, and abandoning their purchases rather than wait.

Which of these relationships would you choose?

Perhaps, in pre-mobile days, Jane would not have looked for that level of ongoing dialogue with her favorite brand. In the old days, customers like Steve might have been willing to endure the wait. But now, they both know better. They know that mobile offers an alternative. That means patience, for what used to be business as usual, is wearing thin.

*It's not you, Retailer. It's me. There was a time when we were happy. But now I want something more.*

The key to the new customer demand is understanding that it's not just a new technology customers want. They want what technology has the power to deliver – a new and improved customer relationship.

Customer relationships have long been part of the retail equation. In the pre-mobile days, that relationship was built and nurtured in large part through service. Retailers often used customer service as a point of differentiation. Walmart stationed greeters at the door. Nordstrom sales staff were trained in the art of attentive service. Chain stores schooled associates to greet customers and offer them assistance as they moved through the store. There was a time when such customer service was enough to make many shoppers happy. If the customer was treated with respect and attention and received "service with a smile," that in many cases translated to a stellar retail experience. Great retailers gave great service as a way to distinguish themselves in the marketplace. Elite brands took service to extreme lengths and commanded high prices for their efforts. Customers of these brands could expect personalized service and staff who would learn their likes and dislikes and serve them over many years.

In the mobile age, customers demand more from their relationships. eMarketer found that when customers interact with brands, 81% expect all their questions to be answered, 52% are looking for personalized service, and 57% consider a service mistake a reason to switch brands[4].

# Customers Demand More...

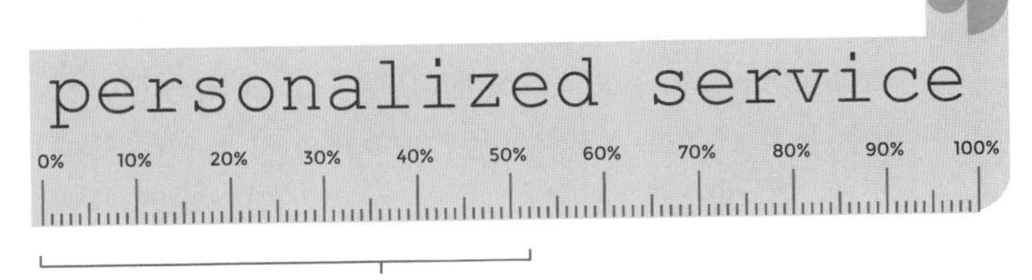


**52%**

of customers are looking for personalized service.

**81%**

expect all questions to be answered.

**57%**

consider a service mistake a reason to switch brands.

Source: eMarketer, How to Win at Customer Service: Keep It Simple, October, 2015

Service is not the gold standard; it's a basic expectation, and just one of many. Awakened by technology to the possibilities, the customer knows a rich and full experience is possible, beyond just service, which now seems a small part of their customer journey. This encompasses much more than a smile and a thank you. It's a robust buffet of options, offers, opportunities, and services the customer is learning to expect in the retail arena. This poses a new challenge to the retail community, not because it has failed to execute its customer service mission, but because technology has opened the portal to new possibilities. The definition of what good service is has changed and grown to include more than just working with an associate in a store.

This is hardly the first time retail has faced a challenge to the status quo. Mom-and-pop stores battled big-box discounters. Downtowns faced off against suburban malls. Stores were pummeled by the web. It's a familiar cycle to the industry. Now mobile presents a new battleground for retailers, but this time around, there's a shift in attitude on the part of the retail community. In previous eras, retailers might have met a challenge with price wars and other traditional defensive moves. This time around, retailers are showing their willingness to reexamine relationships. Rather than playing defense, a vanguard section of the industry is facing the challenge not to battle but to transform. Retailers are coming to realize they must meet customers where they are – on the small screen – and deliver the shopping experience they are coming to expect.

## The Age of Customer Engagement

What does a transformed customer relationship look like? It begins with a high level of engagement.

"Engagement" is a term sometimes employed by the technology industry. It can be used to describe the outcome of a formula, an equation of attention plus time plus action that is designed to reveal how effective a technology has been in influencing its desired customers.

Engagement in the wider business community has relationship implications. It describes the new relationship the customer wants and not just with retailers but with the many product, service, and entertainment options available. Engagement is a deeper level of connection. The bond is deeper, stronger, and from the customer's point of view, more satisfying.

That satisfaction is driving change at retail and, really, across industries. Customers are unwilling to settle for any brand, any service, any product, that doesn't offer engagement. In a contest between a brand that engages and a brand that does not, the choice is simple. Engagement wins.

This puts the burden on all brands to be engaging. The challenge is amplified by the requirement to create engaging experiences via the small screen, and many brands are hesitant: only 14% say they are using mobile to transform the customer experience[5].

How do you create customer engagement in mobile settings? Early adopters are already paving the way with the following techniques.

# The Age of Mobile Customer Engagement

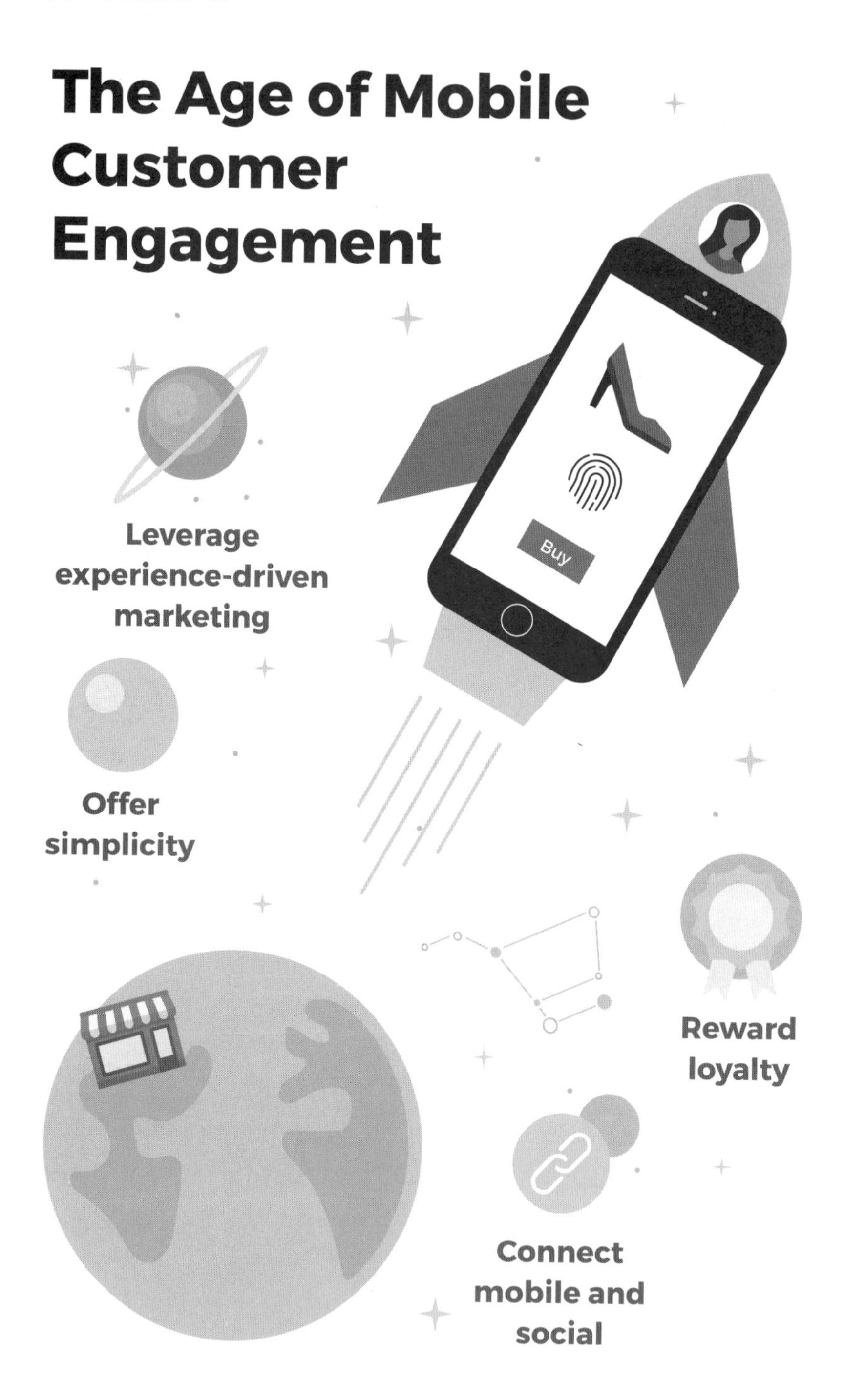

### They Offer Simplicity

In a complex and fast-moving world, consumers appreciate a brand that promises to simplify their lives. As brands seek to transform their relationships for the mobile age, they should look to their own wares and ask: does this make my customer's life simpler? If the answer is yes, the potential for a positive relationship comes into view. In our *Mobile Retail Report*, we found this to be an area of opportunity for many retailers. The ease of search, select, and buy via the app resulted in an average of 5.9 clicks or taps to complete the purchase with 20 fields (on average) being required. This is far too much effort being imposed on customers in their mobile journeys.

Meanwhile, brands delivering simplicity are already making themselves known in mobile commerce. Consider the example of HotelTonight, a hotel booking app that connects last-minute travel customers with hotels that have empty rooms about to go unfilled. No question, the element of "last minute" already suggests a consumer with a looming deadline who does not have time to wander around online, clicking and waiting for pages to load and filling out long registration pages. This consumer needs a place to lay her head. The app with the simple approach will be appealing.

HotelTonight delivers with a smooth user experience. The app provides a platform that offers speedy payment and stored user payment information. Returning customers can book a room in 10 seconds with three taps and a swipe. That's about a tenth of the speed of near competitors. Even more important, the process is supremely simple. By delivering simplicity, HotelTonight creates engagement and a positive customer relationship born of mobile technology.

### They Reward Loyalty the Twenty-First-Century Way

Loyalty cards are due for an upgrade. Who's willing to continue carrying around a plastic card in order to demonstrate loyalty and receive rewards? This is about as likely as finding a man who's still carrying a plastic comb in his back pocket.

Still, loyalty matters to the modern shopper. A 2015 survey by SessionM found that 76% of smartphone users would be more likely to choose a brand if a loyalty program were available.

Mobile, therefore, provides a way to continue the profitable practice of loyalty marketing without insisting customers carry a bit of plastic just in case they want to shop. Customer loyalty is a behavioral change that often has little to do with traditional perceptions of loyalty, such as point systems and custom credit cards. Mobile loyalty means offering exclusive experiences, interactions, and products to a brand's best customers. It means nurturing relationships and using impactful techniques to make customers more loyal by making them feel better and different.

Mobile technology allows retailers to deliver exclusive offerings directly to customers. The notifications can be pushed, tailored to individuals, flex with the time of day, and offer truly personalized service, even when customers aren't in the store. In many cases, customers don't even need to install an app thanks to wallet/passbook systems like the one offered by Apple on the iPhone that allows customers to be out in the world yet engaged with the brand.

### They Leverage Experience-Driven Marketing

What if your marketing didn't actually sell your product but rather offered a related experience? The chain called Rituals has 400 stores around the world stocked with luxury spa items from perfumes and makeup to scented candles and gift boxes. But that's not what you'll see in one of their most popular mobile marketing efforts. One of the chain's most successful programs is a collection of content designed to introduce and coach visitors in meditation. The Rituals meditation app is a guided program for meditation beginners and is free. There's nothing visibly for sale save a subtle "shop" link at the top of the screen.

This is marketing that focuses not on the sale or even on the product but on an experience that might well resonate long after customers move on to other aspects of their days. What's more, this experience and the sense of peace and tranquility the app delivers are free! That's more than a sale. It's a way for the brand to connect with consumers, convey it knows what they really want, and present itself as a purveyor not just of stuff people want to buy but of lives they want to live.

That's more than a sales pitch; it's a relationship.

### They Understand the Connection between Mobile and Social

One of the most successful fashion-related series on U.S. television these days is called *Say Yes to the Dress*. Each episode features a bride-to-be trying on wedding dresses under the expert guidance of Randy Fenoli and his team at Kleinfeld Bridal in Manhattan. These individuals present the bride with a series of dresses, she tries them on, and after a suitable amount of indecision and suspense, she says "Yes" to the one she likes the best.

Central to the dramatic narrative of this show is the fact that each bride brings along a handful of close advisors, usually her mother, her sisters, a couple of friends, and for extra tension, her dad. Shopping for a wedding dress is not just an exercise in retail. It's not like going to Walmart to buy towels. This is a social occasion, a chance to bond and share in the joy of one of life's most joyous and cherished events. In other words, the social aspect of shopping for a dress is almost as important as the dress itself. It turns the object into an experience.

That is what retailers, especially those in fashion and luxury goods, must remember. Shopping is a social activity. In many cases, the buyer seeks social approval, and the opinions of those trusted friends are vital to the decision.

You might object that not every shopper is going to arrive at your store with half a dozen family members and friends in tow, but mobile commerce technology is in fact making this happen, heightening the in-store shopping experience by making it a social event. When shoppers look to buy items that connect in some way to personal taste and style, they often seek the approval and guidance of others. This habit reflects our natural tribal instincts. Consumers who can scan an item and show it off to a friend or a few friends by way of a live video smartphone connection give the retailer a set of golden keys.

As shoppers and their friends search for items they're interested in purchasing, the store's clienteling tools can help. The sales associate can act as a guide and expert. At the same time, the friends can be brought more fully into the store's inner circle by being shown a range of items they might not have considered for themselves, and of course they can be invited to download the store's app.

As customers move more and more toward mobile, store owners must dispense with the myth that mobile is a technical choice.

## Engagement Is Always On

The good news for brands is that while customers are demanding this intense new relationship, they are willing to give as well as receive. Engaged customers take their positive view of your brand everywhere they travel in the mobile universe. Satisfied customers with strong relationships act as brand ambassadors in the social media community. These engaged customers can be prompted to share on social media, to discuss the brand in online and offline communities, and to represent the brand with other customers. It's a reward for the time, effort, and money the brand might shell out in order to offer something great customers can't get elsewhere.

Finally, the new rules of customer engagement mean there's no disengagement. The purchase does not conclude the relationship. Most retailers view a purchase – whether an in-store sale that culminates with the customer walking out with a bag full of merchandise or an electronic sale that sends the order to a warehouse for fulfillment – as the end point in their omnichannel commerce strategy. In our *Mobile Retail Report*, we found that 79% of customers received personalized communication from the retailer after an online purchase but only 1% of customers received communication from the retailer after an in-store purchase. The opportunity for more engagement is obvious. A sale is just the tip of the iceberg. It's the start of a relationship that is potentially long in time frame and wide in scope.

Much attention is placed on customer analytics, targeted selling, and customized offers as techniques for extending relationships. An equally important component of the strategy is delivery. Amazon built its early success by making delivery fast and easy. This means finding the quickest and in many cases the cheapest way to get the purchase to the customer. The possibility of fulfilling an order with inventory that exists on the premises, in a store across town, or in a warehouse across the country is a lateral expansion of the relationship. It will ultimately drive new store formats, new job categories for retailers, and inventive, individualized delivery solutions such as Deliv and UberRUSH.

## *The Old Store Is Dead; Long Live the New Store*

Shortly after Amazon launched, commerce pundits of the era began predicting the downfall of physical retail stores. "Why would consumers ever walk into a store when they could order everything they need from the comfort of their own homes?" they asked.

The commerce thought leaders of today have a more enlightened view. They realize that shopping can be entertaining and multisensory. They know it is inherently social and self-driven. They also know that some aspects of a physical store are nearly impossible to replicate virtually. This includes touching an item, discovering other items close by, experiencing a store's overall look and feel, and trying the fit and feel of everything from clothes to shoes to fishing rods to books to cars and more. Research by Boston Retail Partners found that despite the rise of new technology, 90% of transactions still occur in stores[6].

This is not to say there won't be changes, many of which will be strongly influenced by mobile. As the relationship between brands and customers is redefined, the impact of mobile becomes clear. The experience leads customers to reevaluate their relationships with brands and to form bonds with those that meet their new, mobile-elevated standards. Customers have embraced mobile. Many retailers and brands are already experimenting with the technology. As the rest of the industry follows, engaged shoppers will vote with their thumbs and wallets for the relationships that truly make them happy.

## *To Wrap Up:*

- Simplify. Mobile users seek brands that make their lives easier. Look for ways your mobile offering will deliver simplicity to attract and engage customers.
- Strive for a dialogue. Since users carry their smartphones everywhere, the opportunity for ongoing conversations is possible. Take advantage and look for ways to engage customers and share their days.
- Think engagement, not just conversion. The sale is just the start. Now, customers are never far from your store. They're probably looking at their mobile screens right now! Successful mobile brands create opportunities and reasons for customers to engage even after the sale has been made.

## *Next Steps:*

- Observe your customers. At what stage of mobile readiness are they? Are they already using mobile technology in other aspects of their lives? How can you simplify your customers' lives by offering a mobile app? This is an important first step. As a retailer, you want to introduce a process that will please customers, not confound them. When you set out to observe, you might find that your customers are more eager for mobile engagement than you have anticipated.

- Conduct an audit of your existing technologies. What technology are you currently using in stores, and how well is it working? Do you have a functional ecommerce system that needs to be connected to a mobile option, or are you starting from scratch to build a virtual business? Know what tech is already at work in your system and how it can be leveraged for mobile transformation.
- Assess your organizational readiness. How ready is your staff for a mobile transformation? Are your store associates already using mobile devices on their own time? Are they ready to learn mobile strategies for use on the job? What about the rest of your organization? Are you in a position to share information between departments? Can your organization work as a whole, without silos, to transform for the mobile age?
- Define your mobile strategy. What do you want from a mobile program? Are you hoping to boost sales? Improve conversions? Is this a marketing communications platform? A tool for associates? Think about what you want from the technology before you launch it.

## Voices from the Mobile Makeover

*Daren Hull, SVP Technology, Stores, and West Elm Digital at Williams-Sonoma, Inc. (former Chief Operating Officer at Outdoor Voices)*

For Daren Hull, the impetus to go mobile starts with customers. Customers, he says, don't use smartphones as simply another piece of technology. The relationship between user and mobile is far more personal. "Remember how you felt the last time you lost yours, broke it, or left it at home," he says. It's that personal relationship that must permeate retailers' adoption of the technology.

Already, Outdoor Voices uses mobile in its point-of-sale and service systems in physical stores and also has made its website responsive for mobile browsing. But much more in mobile is coming. Hull predicts, "[Mobile] will continue to grow in importance as a way to directly engage our consumers in our brand and a way to be part of their lives. It is our most important touch point for marketing, clienteling, and service."

Expanding mobile usage is not without challenges, he allows. Coping with legacy technology and architecture slows the process, and slow is one thing mobile customers will not tolerate. These customers demand speed.

Retailers, Hull says, can ill afford to miss the mobile shift. After all, it's already changing the business landscape. He explains, "Mobile has changed customers, and at a much faster pace than websites did back in the '90s. Look at how quickly a brand like Starbucks earned $1B in transactions through its app. It's not just a download; it drives a core piece of business and interaction with consumers. From payments to loyalty, from delivery to clienteling, mobile will be one of the greatest enablers in coming years, but in different ways than we do business today." He concludes, "You need to start solving your customer experience challenges of tomorrow, today."

*Chapter 2*

# The Store Relationship Makeover

**Insights**

- Stores are not dead; they are ready for mobile makeovers.
- Shoppers are already carrying their phones into stores. Smart stores are flipping that into an opportunity.

## *Are stores in trouble?*

Some suggest the rise of technology-assisted shopping will hurt stores, but that might be a hasty judgment. Stores, rather than being threatened by technology, will be enhanced by it. Mobile is not the end of stores but rather part of the evolution of stores as they transform for the mobile age.

## *Change Is Part of Retailing*

Many things in the U.S. retail world have been retired to the history books, from the door-to-door salesman to cash on delivery.

The store is different. Ever since the early days of the internet, industry watchers have put the store on death-watch. Ecommerce would kill the store, they warned. Not so much.

Not only has the store survived, but smart stores can get in on the new technology and thrive. We've seen stores venture onto the web to challenge Amazon, but the opportunity doesn't end there. As mobile has flipped the shopping cart, new opportunities for traditional stores have emerged. The store, far from being dead or in the process of dying, might just be getting started.

The trick, smart retailers are noticing, is not to focus the battle on beating ecommerce at its game. Amazon is a powerful force in the retail world, and shoppers are well trained to its top-notch execution of convenience and low prices. Smart stores have ecommerce sites but are branching into technology that allows them to score wins, not ties, with pure ecommerce players. In many cases, that technology is mobile.

Mobile offers traditional retailers a unique opportunity to flip the script and battle back (particularly against Amazon) in the war for the hearts and minds of shoppers. While websites might have made inroads, traditional retail stores have elements they alone can leverage to secure shopper dollars. Often, these are battles stores can win.

Let's look at just some of the options for the mobile-savvy traditional retailer.

## In-Store Wi-Fi

Nearly all shoppers have experienced that moment of horror born of the realization that their smartphone plans are running out of data and might not be able to power the next RetailMeNot coupon search or quick Facebook Messenger conversation. This easily addressed problem has prompted several brands to implement a customer-friendly solution: complimentary in-store Wi-Fi. Often the greatest challenge facing stores is getting customers to cross the threshold. Customers might slow as they pass the attractive window display, might peer into the open door, might glance at a sign or two promising discounts, but many stores need help making that last pitch and successfully enticing them to enter. For mobile-carrying customers, Wi-Fi can be that powerful lure.

Subway is one brand that's betting on it. Consumers who walk into a Subway restaurant can pull out their mobile devices and connect to the designated free Wi-Fi network whose landing page prompts them to sign in via text message, Facebook, or email. Once sign-in is complete, individuals receive a mobile coupon from Subway redeemable for a free sandwich. This gives them even more incentive to stay at the restaurant for an extended period of time and also to tell their friends and family about the promotion. Perhaps most rewardingly, the brand enjoys a mobile win by gaining that customer's personal data, allowing it to follow up with additional offers and news in the future, potentially transforming that person from a Subway agnostic to a Subway superfan. Furthermore, retailers that enact this strategy with the proper in-store signage can inspire a plethora of non-targeted consumers to venture inside and potentially purchase some unexpectedly desirable merchandise.

# The Mobile-Savvy Retailer

Welcome Carrie, let me know if you need help.

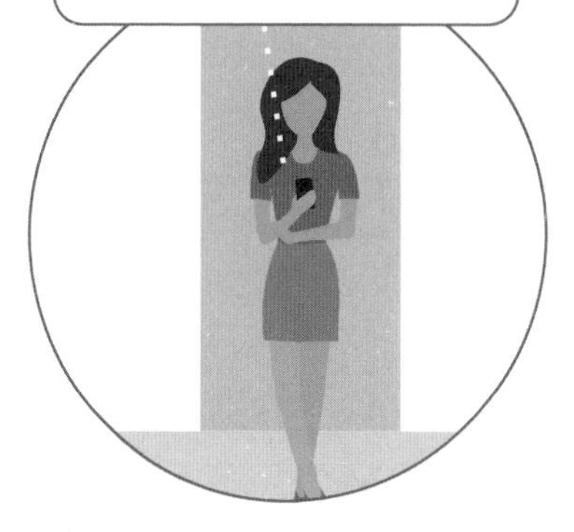

Customer enters the store.

Alert: Carrie has entered the store.

Store associate receives push notification.

Carrie, a shirt on this rack matches your new jeans and shoes!

Customer gets automated in-store recommendations helped by proximity beacons.

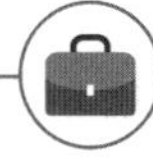

Added handbag to your wishlist!

Customer scans product to wishlist with smartphone.

The use of in-store Wi-Fi can also be a boon to sales staff. In a boutique, for example, once the in-store Wi-Fi has enticed a customer to enter, the store associate is now armed to be of service. Does the customer want to know if the shoes she likes are available in another color? Or if there's a matching handbag? A mobile-enabled store associate can answer that question in seconds. The mobile device offers additional ways for that store associate to serve the customer. She can deliver personalized discounts on the spot. She can also arrange delivery, everything from same day via UberRUSH to overnight via postal service. Our *Mobile Retail Report* revealed that only 38% of the stores we audited offered free Wi-Fi in the store and only 4% of retailers had an associate who recommended an app download while the customer was in the store. Wi-Fi is an area of opportunity. The computer in the shopper's hand is a powerful asset because in-store Wi-Fi appeals to busy shoppers.

## In-Store Services

Many retailers are evolving their business models to include an emphasis on styling and other in-store services, reflecting the need to offer add-on shopping experiences that fuel consumers to shop at their stores instead of at Amazon. The mobile device plays a key role in these service offerings. Stores design the experiences to be marketed and sold via the small screen.

# In-Store Services

Only

**38%**

of stores offer free
Wi-Fi in-store.

Only

**4%**

of retailers had an associate that recommended an app download while in-store.

Source: NewStore, 2016
Mobile Retail Report

As an example, Sephora is now letting its app users schedule makeup application lessons and makeovers directly from their smartphones. Consumers can locate their nearby Sephora store and indicate whether they'd like to book a custom makeover session that requires a product purchase of $50 or more, or a complimentary 15-minute mini-makeover if they're a loyalty program member. Once the desired session has been selected, users can choose their preferred appointment day and time.

By making this offering mobile friendly, rather than offering it via a desktop website, Sephora shows it understands the day-to-day lives of its customers. Certainly, the makeover session might be something customers schedule in advance, but it's just as likely to be a spur-of-the-moment decision, something shoppers and their friends decide to try out one day while perusing the stores. Sephora shows it understands the many ways it interacts with its customers, and it uses mobile not to replace its stores but to enhance them. Mobile becomes the method for making its stores even more successful.

Retailers with significant mobile-savvy fan bases can perfect their omnichannel commerce efforts by enabling consumers to request services on their smartphones. For example, busy individuals who don't have the necessary time to order an outfit online for an upcoming event should have the ability to book an evening styling appointment at a favorite apparel store. Sephora's example should also be followed by marketers with strong loyalty programs. Offering a free custom mini-makeover or similar service to reward program members can be especially successful in convincing them to stop by and browse new products, even if they hadn't planned to do so.

But services needn't be that complicated. Staples is now testing an interactive map delivered through its app designed to help shoppers who know what they want grab and go rather than having to browse the store floor or search for a sales associate. At Zara, shoppers can scan barcodes using their mobile phones to bring up additional product information through the store's app.

## Mobile Self-Checkout

This is a way in which mobile can solve a major store headache – the checkout line. No one likes waiting in line, and it's especially frustrating when you've spent time browsing, choosing items, perhaps trying on a number of outfits. You're happy with your selection and ready to take out your credit card and then – oh, no! – the checkout line looms. In many stores, retailers use a nylon rope to guide shoppers through the maze of waiting to approach the cash register. This imbues the checkout process with all the allure of the TSA airport experience and can easily serve to undo any positive vibes that might have previously existed. In fact, it's not uncommon for customers to make a selection, see a long line at checkout, and decide, "Never mind." Perhaps those customers go home and make the same purchase via ecommerce, but it's just as likely they give up on the whole notion. Brands that worry about abandoned shopping carts online should be just as worried about abandoned purchases at the store checkout line. In a busy world, waiting in line is a hassle and imposition.

As consumers search for even more ways to maximize their time – especially while shopping – retailers must serve up additional conveniences that make in-store experiences slightly less of a hassle, particularly during peak times. IKEA is working on an answer to this by rolling out a new mobile app in France that enables in-store shoppers to scan desired products with their smartphones' cameras before placing them in the cart. Once all items have been picked up, the app calculates the total and generates a unique QR code that consumers can scan at the checkout counter instead of spending additional time scanning each product. This allows IKEA to leverage mobile to make its stores more attractive.

Amazon is also addressing this issue with its Amazon Go grocery project and "Just walk out" technology. Customers walk in, select food from the shelves, and never have to wait in a checkout line. By tapping their cellphones on a turnstile as they enter, they connect to the store's network and their own Amazon account. Sensors track selected items. When customers leave, the chosen items are added up and their Amazon accounts are charged for the purchases.

## Showrooming

Showrooming occurs when a customer enters a brick-and-mortar store and eyeballs the merchandise but ultimately makes a purchase via some other platform such as a website. This is a process traditional retail has been taught to fear, but smart retailers can use mobile to transform the process into a positive for the store.

Most shoppers – as many as 90% – carry their smartphones into stores. Savvy retailers can use that opportunity to deliver personalized discounts, virtual service, and other elements via mobile to entice customers to buy now, not later. For example, a smartphone can be used to deliver brand information via barcode scanning while telling a product story.

Retailers can also make use of technology such as beacons to know when loyal customers enter a store, what their buying history has been, and what previous offers they have found most appealing. So far, only a handful of retailers are doing so. Beacons hold great promise, but brands are not yet making these investments and implementing relevant uses. Still, the potential is there.

Imagine that a customer enters a store with the intention of showrooming. He's planning to look around, make a mental decision, and then go home and buy via Amazon or another web store that has the cheapest price. But wait – as he's shopping, a targeted offer appears via the store's app on his mobile screen offering a great deal. Plus, the app offer explains he can opt for any number of delivery arrangements, including having the item delivered to his home via a service such as UberRUSH later that evening. With all of his shopping problems solved, why wait? He makes his purchase in the store.

### *The Goal: Streaming Retail*

After incorporating these elements, smart stores can begin bringing them all together in a system we call streaming retail. Remember the TV listings section of the newspaper detailing what was going to be on TV that day? Advertisers generally paid much higher rates to place ads on the TV page than anywhere else in the paper, except for the comics page.

After all, this guide told you when a show was going to air and on what channel. If you wanted to see it, you had to be there.

Although broadcast TV still thrives today, more and more viewers are choosing to watch shows from on-demand streaming services such as Netflix, or to watch broadcast episodes later through TV network apps. That's where TV is going. There's a smooth transition between the various media, and there's a much higher degree of interactivity, with episodes and shows encouraging simultaneous conversations on social media.

This streaming approach is a must-have for retail. Think about it: streaming connotes flow. It's not a stop-and-go approach. In the old world of TV, stop and go meant parking yourself in front of your TV at 8:00 p.m. or missing your show. You had to wait for the commercial breaks to go get a snack. Streaming means you can watch a show on your living room TV whenever you like and can also pick it up on your smartphone as you go to the kitchen to get a sandwich or feed the cat.

Home Depot is one retailer that's on the ball when it comes to streaming shopping with mobile commerce. Home Depot shoppers typically don't wander or browse unless they're lost. A Home Depot shopper says, "I've got a pipe that burst" or "I have a project I'm working on." These are intelligent, product-focused shoppers looking for something specific, so it's not surprising that Home Depot offers an app that allows them to determine where they are in the store while building a product list and determining that the desired parts are in stock. This supports the idea of streaming retail: that people can slide into a store, pick up all the pieces they need, and move on, with minimal detours, delays, or distractions.

Retailers in fashion and elsewhere need to pick up on this idea that shopping is actually a streaming activity for many of their consumers. Many shoppers want to check inventory levels before venturing out to a store so their eventual trip is not in vain. They might request the items be available for pickup by a certain time, or they might expect a well-versed sales associate to walk alongside them like a personal assistant, setting up the items based on a pre-loaded awareness of their tastes.

And why not? That's what shopping has become, and it's a good thing. Retailers must stop thinking of their stores as large boxes of merchandise that shoppers take a chance on. They are in-person fulfillment centers that can and should leverage data as a means of maximizing the retail relationship and minimizing inconvenience in a way that hasn't been done before.

## *The "Wow!" Store, Powered by Mobile*

If Home Depot understands streaming retail, other retailers clearly understand the way mobile can work in concert with retail to create a stellar shopping experience. Consider the Apple retail space, which is a stunning visual example of the vision of Apple Founder Steve Jobs. Jobs, the leading light at Apple, still one of the most successful and valuable companies on the planet, is famous for a lot of radical ideas and innovations. One of his most significant contributions involves the retail consumer experience. Looking beyond smartphones, tablets, and computers to observe the experience of purchasing and owning Apple devices reveals the magic and power of the retailing relationship. Apple stores create a sense of community. People come to explore, test and discuss the product, and speak with associates. Consequently, store design and layout are conducive to community browsing, socializing, and sharing.

One of Jobs's most famous comments, circa 1997, was, "You've got to start with the customer experience and work backwards to the technology." To that end, even before it's activated, Apple's iPhone is an experiential marvel. Delivered in a perfect box, a work of packaging brilliance, the texture, weight, and mechanics of the box hint at the sensory comfort and ease of use of the phone itself. Apple's design team put serious thought into the materials and assembly of this item, something many other manufacturers dismiss as merely a box. It's not an overstatement to say this box delivers a haptic experience that contributes enormously to the overall enjoyment of the purchase. Steve Jobs wouldn't have had it any other way.

Expand this concept to the world of brick-and-mortar. You can see the same experiential ideas built into the physical Apple stores, whose layouts eliminate traditional retail elements such as cash registers and physical shopping carts. Apple has removed an entire middle layer of the retail experience, one that is quickly turning into dead weight in traditional stores as shoppers become more mobile. Apple has shortened the path from discovery to checkout while enhancing the experience.

Take this concept one level higher and observe Apple's sales associates, all of whom seem to be dedicated enthusiasts of Apple products and who act as assistants, experts, and cash points, all armed with mobile devices that allow them to handle any customer request on the spot. There is no checkout. There is no definite finality to the store.

Customers enter and experience. Even the store's famous approach to service via appointments demonstrates the intimate connection between customer, technology, associate, and store.

Not every store needs to emulate the clean, bright lines of Apple, but retailers everywhere should take note of how this particular store redefines the retail experience. Obviously, the Apple store sells its own products, but it would be easy to imagine an offshoot of the Apple Corporation dedicated solely to designing retail experiences for stores of all types, ranging from home hardware to apparel and everything in between.

## *Stores Are Stepping up to the Challenge*

Many retailers are starting to get the mobile message:

- When Barneys New York revamped its Chelsea flagship, the mobile imprint was everywhere: it debuted an iBeacon platform with its mobile app that alerts users to new content and offers to help navigate the store; it pushed editorial content from *The Window*, Barneys' in-house publication, to customer phones, including new seasonal lookbooks, designer interviews, and videos; and it put mobile devices into the hands of every salesperson to better personalize the shopping experience. In stores, sales associates armed with iPhones have access to real-time inventory, allowing associates to check on the availability of any item, in any size, all without walking away from the customer. Whether Barneys' mobile efforts will succeed in the long run isn't known, but these are important steps in the journey.

- Macy's has looked for ways to use mobile technology to enhance the in-store experience. The retailer installed a beacon system in 800+ stores, developed a shopping app, and added Apple Pay to its point-of-sale devices. Most recently, the retailer partnered with IBM's Watson to develop an AI mobile shopping assistant tool. In early tests, this virtual assistant, accessible to customers via their mobile devices, allows them to ask questions such as directions to a certain brand or department within a given store. A Spanish-language version is also in development. The goal, says Macy's, is to improve the customer shopping experience and free up store associates to cater to more complicated shopper needs.
- Target launched Cartwheel, a mobile coupon app that provides in-store coupons and other special offers to shoppers in stores using beacon technology to convey the whereabouts of these items.

What's more, research suggests mobile options in stores could appeal to some of the most desirable customers. A 2015 research report from DMI titled "Shoppers Want More from in-Store Mobile" found that the highest-value audience – a group termed Mobile Reliants – showed the strongest interest in in-store mobile shipping tools such as instant price and inventory check and mobile self-checkout[7].

## Technology Can Add Luxury to Any Store

Ultimately, the goal of every traditional retail store should be to leverage technology – mobile and otherwise – to refine, enhance, and deliver the element we all seek when we engage in commerce: a pleasurable retail experience. A critical route to defining the best retail experience is the adoption of technology that either makes existing shopping excursions better or that provides new ones. For brands driven mostly by discounts, this might be about enabling a monetary type of reward. For others, it might be through an app that delivers early or exclusive access to a sale.

For forward-thinking retailers, technology can inject an elevated customer experience into an otherwise mundane shopping trip. Consider those customers who are fond of particular coffee combinations. Typically, they enter the store of their choice and order it every day. Smart stores will offer these customers the opportunity to download their store apps and record their regular orders. As these individuals leave their homes for work, they can submit their personal orders and, a short drive later, find them waiting, freshly prepared, when they pull into the drive-through. Now the daily coffee run carries an element of luxury. The coffee hasn't changed, but mobile technology makes consumers feel like the center of their store's universe.

Each brand has the opportunity to develop new relationships in ways that wouldn't be possible without technology. When you look at what people want from retailers, it isn't merely discounts. They want value adds such as content or experiences.

This is the retailing relationship in action. In an age where so much can be purchased online, the aesthetic pleasure of a well-planned, technologically integrated store makes the price and effort worthwhile.

Stores are not dead. They are only getting started. Mobile is taking them to new levels of service and customer satisfaction. Why would anyone want to sit home on the couch?

## *To Wrap Up:*

- Stores are not dead; they are poised for a mobile transformation. Far too many people say technology will mean the end of stores, but in fact, most retail transactions still take place in traditional stores. Shoppers are in no hurry to abandon stores entirely. The advent of technology is not the end of stores but the beginning of a new customer-centric store experience.
- Mobile + Stores = Happy, Engaged Customers. Stores that are already using mobile in their physical locations are seeing the benefits. Walk around any Apple store, and you'll see customers engaging with Apple staffers armed with mobile devices. Mobile technology allows staffers to go to new heights in serving and delighting customers, up to and including handling the mobile-enabled no-line checkout.
- The omnichannel experience – streaming retail – is the future of commerce. Customers are already comfortable toggling between their devices and the physical world, and they expect retail to adapt to this reality. It's no longer acceptable to tell a customer that policies or selection differs depending on how they shop; customers expect a seamless experience. Omnichannel is already the expectation, and smart retailers will embrace it as their reality.

## Next Steps:

- Have working Wi-Fi in your store. It's the least you can do. Everyone who comes through the door will have a mobile device.
- Research what luxury means to your customers. How can you create a luxury experience for them?
- Think outside the box. What experiments can you implement in your store to delight customers?
- Look for ways mobile can enhance the store experience. Can it boost the output of store associates? Can it offer instant discounts? Can it bust the checkout line? Mobile is not a threat but an opportunity to introduce customer-centric service.
- Consider whether or not your associates should use shared mobile devices or their own personal mobile devices on the job.
- Watch leaders like Apple and learn from how they bridge the gap between channels using technology.
- Hire mobile-minded talent in retail jobs. The savvier your staff, the more successful your mobile transformation will be.

## Voices from the Mobile Makeover

*Ted McNamara, CFO and Treasurer, M.Gemi*

Mobile is a major factor in Ted McNamara's luxury retail business. Almost two-thirds of his online traffic comes from mobile devices, but don't expect him to ditch the physical for the virtual anytime soon. "We are big fans of physical retail," he says. The key is to integrate the power and attraction of mobile into the store.

To that end, M.Gemi's new NYC store is packed with the latest mobile technology. iPad minis are available for customer and associate use. Mobile card reading is available for checkout. And store associates can use mobile technology to better connect with the customers who come in by viewing their shopping histories.

The mistake retailers make when looking at mobile and other technologies is failing to appreciate the different positives each retail platform can bring to the customer experience. Not all channels can do all things well. "We use our stores for exploration, for brand storytelling, for a deeper engagement with the customer," McNamara says. "We use online for selling, for service, for delivery and logistics." Rather than thinking in omnichannel terms, he says, his company thinks of channels as complementary.

What's coming next? Changes in the way retailers communicate with customers. "Most ecommerce businesses are still heavily reliant on email," McNamara explains, "but email is sometimes difficult to read on a phone." He says, "We are looking at other ways people use their phones, and so we look for new ways to engage. Whether it's RSS or Facebook Messenger or other technology, those changes in communication are the next wave."

Chapter 3

# The Associate Relationship Makeover

**Insights**

- Associates want to use mobile to better serve their customers and to be more successful at their jobs.
- Associates know more than management about how mobile works and would need little training to operate an app.

The following paragraph is taken from an actual posted job description. See if you can guess what it's for.

> *Successful applicant will demonstrate efficient and effective use of tablet, mobile and smartphone technology to drive sales. Share product features and benefits by using vendor QR codes, online reviews and social media apps. Skills necessary: Demonstrated proficiency with computers, tablets, smartphones and associated apps, programs and social media tools. Interest in and ability to learn new technology skills.*

Based on this description, who would you say is hiring? A mobile marketing agency? An ecommerce start-up?

This is an ad for a Macy's store associate. For this very visible customer service job, Macy's doesn't just want someone who knows how to sell. It wants this person to be technology proficient. It wants someone who already understands that mobile has flipped the shopping cart.

This is significant because it signals one of the great makeovers that must take place if retail is to transform for the mobile age – the makeover of the store associate. Far too often, it's assumed the transformation to mobile is a technical experience that will play out on screens, in IT departments, and via algorithms. The truth is, the power of the mobile makeover will be apparent in the most common everyday human experiences of retailing. As retail transforms for the mobile age, store associates will be a vital part of the process.

## *Mobile Transformation Must Start in Stores*

It might seem obvious that store associates must participate in the transformations of their stores, but if you walk into many stores today and look around, you might think mobile hadn't been invented yet. In most stores, you'll see plenty of desktops at the point-of-sale. You might even see screens in other public-facing departments such as customer service or returns. But you can cruise the floor for hours in most major retailers without seeing a single associate with a mobile device in his or her hand. Our *Mobile Retail Report* revealed that only 33% of retailers had mobile devices in use by their associates; about two-thirds of the associates had visibility into customers' past purchases.

If retailers seem to think their stores should be mobile-free zones, it's clear their customers disagree. While associates might have parked their phones in the break room, shoppers are carrying them onto the sales floor. They've got them in hand when they browse, cross-check prices, post to social media, and chat with friends. As far as shoppers are concerned, entering a store is no reason to turn off their smartphones; our research suggests that 90% of shoppers not only have their mobile devices with them in stores but also use them [in stores][8].

If this is the case, why are so many store associates empty-handed? The answer is simple: many retailers still manage their associates like it's 1999.

This fact stems from what used to pass for top-notch customer service in the century gone by. In the pre-mobile era, customer service had a great deal to do with eye contact. Human beings value eye contact and judge others based on it, so store associates were trained to look customers in the eye, smile, and say, "Welcome!" After all, a person who is looking at you cares about you. For sure, a service employee who doesn't look at you must be ignoring you!

It stands to reason that retailers not only trained their employees to make eye contact but also punished those who didn't. Because associates were reviewed and compensated based on their ability to connect with customers, the mobile phone was assumed to pose a threat to the promise of great customer service. How could an associate offer good customer service while looking at a small screen?

# Mobile Devices In-Store

## 90%

of shoppers use their mobile devices in stores.

But only

## 33%

of retailers had mobile devices in use by their associates.

## 67%

of the associates had visibility into a customer's past purchases.

Source: NewStore, 2016 Mobile Retail Report; "The Store Associate Dilemma: Mobile Enablement, So Close Yet So Far," NewStore Webinar

Consequently, rules sprang up quickly in the advent of the mobile era. Upper management equated cell phone usage with goofing off, so associates weren't allowed to even have their mobile phones on the job, let alone use them. Cell phones would distract employees, and customers would be put off by the sight of associates gazing into the palms of their hands rather than making eye contact.

## *Associates Would Love to Go Mobile*

This attitude had a significant impact on associates' workdays. As noted, only 33% use mobile devices on the job. If you're a member of upper management, this might seem like a good thing. Perhaps you imagine you've cleared your associates to better do their jobs. In fact, a mobile-free sales floor is a danger sign. Associates who are asked to leave their mobile devices behind are being removed from the customer experience. When customers carry their mobile devices into the store but associates have been forced to leave theirs behind, it creates a disconnect.

Imagine that a customer walks in and asks about a product promoted in an app. If the associate has no access to this app, the two now have a problem. These two groups should be in sync in order to execute a great shopping experience. Instead, associates are banned from participating.

Retail management needs to come to terms with a key reality of mobile commerce: store associates are mobile retail transformation's front line. These are the individuals who will take the concept of mobile retail and make it happen in the real world, for real customers. These are the people who will take a retailer from the status of "mobile enabled" to "mobile engaged." These are the two necessary stages in the process of transformation for the mobile age, and it's not unusual to see a company stuck at this juncture. It's often what happens when companies that have put true effort and resources into mobile transformation leave out the crucial last step of the process. Retailers might be "mobile enabled." They might have invested appropriately and hired the right staff and outside vendors to craft and launch mobile shopping, but until they create that moment of connection for customers in the real world, "enabled" falls short of "engaged." Retailers that are mobile engaged have the technology up and running, with the full organization reaping the many benefits of the mobile system.

"Enabled" means you have the ability to execute. It means you're ready. The word "engaged" is active – you're already doing it. Think of this in terms of car ownership. If you own a car, you're transportation enabled, but if you don't know how to drive, that's where the experience ends. You need the skills and also permission to get into that car and drive. Otherwise, the car sits in your driveway, and you're probably frustrated because you've spent a lot of money on that car, yet you're not going anywhere. It's maddening!

That's where many retailers and brands are today – sitting with their mobile-enabled process in their driveways but not yet allowing anyone to drive that brand-new car.

## *Your Associates Can Drive Your Mobile Efforts*

The answer to that problem is associates. When retailers shake off their old-fashioned thinking about mobile phones on the job, they can turn their associates loose to make mobile-carrying customers happy.

Some forward-thinking retailers are doing just that.

At Burberry in Manhattan, assistants work the sales floor armed with mobile technology. They walk around taking orders, answering questions on the spot, and checking inventory. They're also happy to allow customers to use the technology to initiate searches and explore delivery options. They can also handle checkout on the spot, eliminating the need to lug merchandise to the cash register and wait in a long line. The technology is barely noticeable, yet it's always nearby when needed.

Far from being off-putting, the use of the small screen in the retail arena is a plus for today's mobile-enabled shoppers. When retailers show customers they understand their lives, a connection is made. When businesses show they are deeply connected to the things that matter to shoppers, relationships are enhanced. It isn't always an obvious connection. Shoppers aren't necessarily going to be impressed by a big ad campaign that trumpets, "We've gone mobile!" But customers have certainly gone mobile, and if retailers or brands do as well, customers are going to notice.

Consider this scenario: Daniel walks into the flagship store of his favorite brand. He's been here many times before, but this is no small store, and a dozen associates are at work on any given day. On this occasion, he's met soon after he enters by a store associate who greets him by name. This particular associate has served Daniel before. She was notified via a beacon when he entered the store. By the time they meet on the sales floor, she has browsed his most recent buying history and also seen what he was looking at via the mobile app earlier that day. Had this particular associate been on break or not working that day, another associate would have received Daniel's information and helped him.

When Daniel makes his final selections, the associate is able to handle his checkout process via her mobile device without having to move to a point-of-sale counter or a desktop. No waiting in line! As she handles the checkout, she alerts Daniel to the variety of fulfillment options he might choose from – he can take the items with him, have them shipped, or have them delivered that same day to his home or office via UberRUSH. Daniel decides to take one of the items with him to wear that evening and to have the rest delivered later that night. He leaves the store happy, and the associate who helped him increases her Net Promoter Score, which is tied to her bonus, for her successful work.

That's the story of two human beings armed with two mobile devices on the retail sales floor and the mutually positive outcome of their interaction.

Now consider this tale, the story of two people and only one mobile device: Kim enters the flagship store of her favorite brand. She's been here many times before, but this is a big store with a lot of sales associates, and she's never been helped by the same person twice. On this day, she enters and pauses at the doorstep, not sure where she wants to go.

An associate folding T-shirts at the front display looks at her and smiles. "Welcome," he says and then goes back to folding. Kim, scanning the rest of the store, smiles back, still trying to determine where she wants to be.

She begins to wander through the racks and displays. She has her smartphone in her hand, and she takes a picture of an item and sends it to a friend. She posts another to her favorite social media app, then browses the app of another store to see if they've got anything on sale. She doesn't know if this store has an app or not, and it doesn't occur to her to find out.

As she passes another store associate, he makes eye contact with her and says, "Can I help you?" Unsure of what she wants, Kim says she's just browsing. She doesn't want to get caught up in a long sales pitch. The store associate acknowledges her answer and points out that the dresses on the rack she's passing are 25% off – the sign on the rack says as much. Kim, who doesn't care for the color of the dress, says thanks and moves on.

No purchase is made. Kim has no idea that the 25%-off dress is available in her favorite color and in stock in another location. She doesn't know she could make the purchase in one store and have the dress delivered to her via shipping or same day service.

The store associates aren't any happier. Yet another customer has come into the store, moved all the T-shirts on the display, and left without purchasing anything. It's just another slow day.

Neither the store nor the customer wins. An opportunity has been wasted. That's the story of two human beings and one mobile device, and it ends with all parties unfulfilled.

## *Shoppers Appreciate the Mobile-Powered Associate*

Far from being put off by attentive sales staff, research suggests that 90% of shoppers spend more when helped by a knowledgeable sales associate. Shoppers understand the value of a sales associate who knows both the customer and the merchandise, and many say they actively appreciate "smart recommendations" by sales associates. These are opportunities to make customers happier and sales larger[9].

Making store associates mobile powered involves more than a technology play. It involves a full understanding of the cultural impact of mobile. The advent of mobile is a change in the way human beings behave. These are devices we carry with us all the time. We have them at home, at work, at school, and when we travel between these places. The idea that we wouldn't have them with us when we step into a store is crazy – of course we do! Asking store associates to stay in sync with mobile-carrying customers without the benefit of their own mobile devices is largely unfair. Retailers that insist their associates stay out of mobile contact during work hours leave them out of the conversation and experience of their customers. Again, they literally disconnect them, and this is a shame, because the opportunity to make customers happy using mobile technology is right at our fingertips.

## *Mobile Associates Are More Efficient*

Mobile technology does more than make shoppers happy; it makes store employees more effective. Consider American Eagle and the way it's testing mobile technology to service both customers and associates. At American Eagle, the use of mobile begins even before customers enter the store. Opt-in beacon technology allows the retailer to locate the customer lurking outside the door, hesitating about whether or not to go in and browse. At this stage, the associate can't do much from inside the store, but mobile technology, once it locates the customer, can send an instant and personalized offer via the store app.

Once the customer has been enticed to come in, the store associate is alerted and can go to work making that customer happy.

But the service of the mobile technology isn't complete. Rather, the technology continues to provide unseen benefits. The beacon might show, for example, how the customer navigates the store. Taken in bulk, that data can help a manager arrange merchandise and assign associates to cover areas of the store and times of day when customer traffic is most demanding. Mobile makes the work of sales that much more efficient.

What's more, mobile can continue to serve the customer outside the store. More and more, stores are using mobile to engage in "conversational commerce." Nordstrom is doing this with text messaging. Using TextStyle, a shopper can send a private text message with a description or photo of a product to a sales associate. The customer can also make the purchase by replying "buy" and entering a unique code. The transaction is handled using the shopper's account at nordstrom.com. Coach, too, is engaging in conversational commerce, integrating into iMessage and using that to build on its Coachmoji keyboard app to engage with customers.

No one recognizes this potential more than store associates themselves, who know that mobile technology would make them better at their jobs. Consider this fact uncovered in our *Mobile Retail Report*: only 18% of brands have inventory visibility through mobile devices. This means sales associates often have to walk away from customers to determine true availability, which is far from good customer service.

What's more, research shows that nearly half of associates would choose a job based on the ability to use their smartphones on the job[10]. That means mobile technology is more than a customer service tool; it's also a recruiting tool. The best sales associates will go to work for the retailers that give them the best possible tools for success. For associates compensated on commission, the imperative is even stronger. They will gravitate to the employer who offers them the way to make the most money. Who would choose otherwise?

## *Mobile Is Making Inroads*

There is good news emerging in the retail landscape. Overall, forward-thinking brands are starting to loosen their grip on employees' use of technology, allowing staffers to participate in the virtual conversations that are already shaping brands in the virtual world. Lane Bryant changed its policy, backing off the requirement that every tweet receive corporate approval before being sent. The new policy allows employees to use the social media platform to connect with customers. At Lilly Pulitzer, policy now encourages store managers to think of themselves as "shopkeepers" and to use social media to engage in conversations and build relationships.

Naturally, a conversation that starts in the virtual world should be continued when shoppers step into a store. It would be silly to promote one kind of conversation in the virtual world but block it entirely within the four walls of a store, but using mobile to continue the conversation is still far from the norm. As our *Mobile Retail Report* revealed, only 11% of store associates offered a personal mobile number to connect while 12% offered a personal email address.

The ban of the small screen puts retailers *and* associates at a disadvantage. The answer is not to banish mobile devices from the store floor but to embrace them and train associates in their use and rules. Associates who are versed in the art of using mobile devices are likely to perform well. Appropriate training and supervision can ensure the devices are being used in service of customers. To this end, retailers should consider reconfiguring compensation so that it rewards associates for using smartphones to make sales.

**Only**

**18%**

**of brands have inventory visible through mobile devices.**

Source: NewStore, 2016 Mobile Retail Report

We are past the era when "May I help you?" was considered good customer service. Savvy mobile shoppers know perfectly well that a store can be helpful – if it wants to be. As shoppers become more experienced with mobile apps, they will begin to judge businesses that fail to offer this service. What would you think of a modern retailer that lacked a website? You would rightly conclude that store was behind the times and not actively courting your business. Soon, that will be the reputation of retailers without mobile-enabled store associates.

Your store associates can do more than refold T-shirts and operate cash registers. Chances are good they already know how to work mobile technology with lightning speed. Get that car out of the driveway and hit the road.

## *To Wrap Up:*

- You might be mobile ready with the right technology, but if your staff isn't allowed to use mobile on the sales floor, you are not mobile engaged. Don't stop at acquiring technology. Push through until everyone in your company uses it.
- Your store associates are likely already experts at mobile technology. It is not something new you will have to train associates to use; off the job, they no doubt spend hours each day on their own devices. Many might already know which mobile features would make them more effective at their jobs.
- Without mobile options, your best customers and associates will move on. Customers will gravitate to stores that offer more personalized service (which mobile can enable), and top store associates will look for employers who offer the latest tools for success. Mobile has already flipped the shopping cart and encouraged both customers and associates to seek new and better options in their work and personal lives.

## *Next Steps:*

- Assess the readiness of your sales associates. It's important that the technology you deploy match the skills of your associates. What are their current mobile skills? What technologies do they already know, and which ones could they be trained to use?

- Launch your mobile strategy. Include store associates as part of the mobile experience. As stores hope to create a smooth, omnichannel experience for customers, it stands to reason that store associates shouldn't be left out of the transformation.
- Turn associates into brand advocates. Let them put together looks for their regular customers. Let them notify customers about new arrivals through chat functionality.
- Make your compensation process more relevant to associates by adding a gaming component, allowing them see their compensation grow as they make more sales.
- Monitor and track your competitors. It's important to consistently monitor what's going on in the mobile space. You will want to most closely watch your direct competitors, but keep an eye on those who are not in your industry. You might see a tactic you want to adopt in your own space.
- Expand associate training so that it's ongoing rather than a one-time event. Technology changes, and it's reasonable to assume associates will need to be trained on a rolling basis to stay current.

## Voices from the Mobile Makeover

*Scott Lux, Vice President of Digital and Ecommerce, John Varvatos*

Scott Lux can envision a day when store associates use mobile to enhance the customer experience. It would unlock a lot of potential for brands, he says, allowing store associates to do more clienteling and allowing brands to be more nimble and responsive. But like many brands, John Varvatos has not yet deployed mobile tech in stores.

Looking broadly at the retail landscape, Lux sees many challenges facing brands as they approach new technology opportunities such as those offered by mobile. What might be simple for a startup to adopt often presents more challenges to an existing brand. What holds brands back? Challenges include:

- Creating an innovation culture. Lux says, "To be relevant, you have to build a culture around innovation — you have to think like a tech company. But that's a barrier for brands."
- Competing priorities. New technology can find itself in constant competition for funds. That puts brands with existing channels such as physical stores and websites in an ongoing debate. "Which initiative do we fund?" asks Lux. "What is the best use of this capital expenditure?"
- Legacy systems. According to Lux, this is a big issue for retailers. A new company with no legacy systems can jump straight into the new technology. A company with an existing business at retail must make some harder choices that will have ripple effects throughout the company. He says, "Most brands have a point-of-sale system that they don't necessarily love but it works. There has to be a very powerful value proposition to get a brand to move off that system."

*Chapter 4*

# The Loyalty Relationship Makeover

**Insights**

- Loyalty programs, popular and successful in the past, are in need of a mobile flip.
- Smart retailers are moving from a points system to rewards that offer access or community experiences.

For years, loyalty in retail has been synonymous with programs that reward customers based on the frequency and monetary value of their purchases. These rewards usually come in the form of points or cash-back rewards, and customers receive them only after completing a purchase at the register.

Current loyalty programs actually exist outside the customer's shopping journey. These programs are a reward for crossing the finish line, but they do not reflect a true customer-retailer relationship. They worked for a very long time and aren't useless; they're just not robust enough today to meet consumers' evolving expectations. When mobile flipped the shopping cart and raised expectations for the shopping experience, legacy loyalty programs began to show their age.

These programs could be considered the equivalent of "Loyalty 1.0." They're the very basic level of loyalty marketing. Their message is, "Thank you for coming to our store. We hope these points will make you come back." Although such a plan might be more effective than no plan at all, it's a long way from saying, "We care about what you like, we're learning from you, and we're responding with a truly tailored shopping experience." Why should brands seek loyalty when they can aim higher?

Well, why settle for loyalty when you can have love?

## *Love Is the New Loyalty*

Love is not an overstatement. Brands have long sought to create emotionally powered connections with customers. The loyalty marketing industry was based on the idea that customers could feel strongly enough about a brand – thanks in part to rewards – that they would never leave. Moving from loyalty to love, by contrast, seeks to tap positive emotions for a long-term connection to customer and brand. For that to happen, brands need to think about communicating with the customer not just once in a while but at many points during the customer journey.

A customer journey encompasses more than a transaction at checkout. Customers might spend hours across multiple visits, browsing items in a brick-and-mortar store and on the retailer's website. They might also speak with several sales associates, assessing the quality and attentiveness of service before choosing to make a purchase. These types of interactions are outside the scope of most of today's loyalty programs. The current programs do not truly reward customers because they do not first provide retailers with critical information to help nourish the relationship as it happens.

## *New Loyalty Programs Are More Sophisticated*

A new generation of technology and services is emerging that allows retailers to expand their loyalty efforts in a more sophisticated fashion. Mobile technology in particular facilitates customer engagement at all points of the purchase process, from the moment customers begin their research to their first venture into a brick-and-mortar store to the decision to make a purchase, and, later, when they reflect on a purchase and decide to shop again. The next generation of loyalty programs will engage customers and earn their repeat business in a far more personal way. We found in our research for our *Mobile Retail Report* that retailers commonly reward frequent shoppers with loyalty programs and that access to those accounts is provided in 88% of native apps and 94% of mobile websites.

New Balance is a good example. The athletic shoe company has an easily navigable shopping app that provides a direct connection to the company's reward program. When shoppers open this app, they are greeted by individualized rewards information indicating their level of achievement (Silver, Bronze, etc.) and the number of NB points earned. This reminds consumers that they are invested in the New Balance brand.

What can mobile do for loyalty?

# What Can Mobile Do for Loyalty?

**It can deliver experiences rather than loyalty points.**

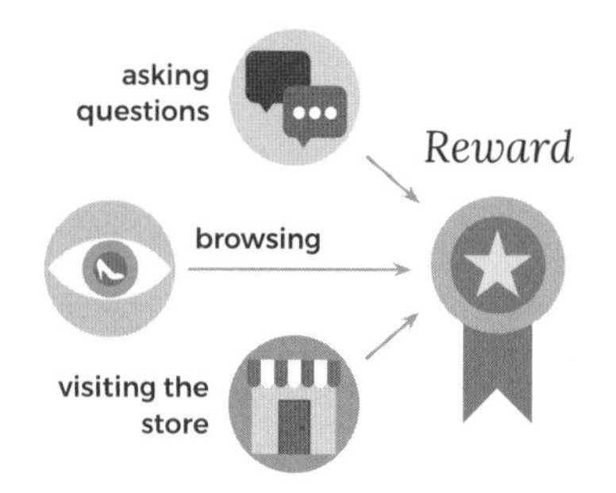


**It can take advantage of all engagement drivers.**

**It can make the transaction itself a loyalty driver!**

### It Can Deliver Experiences Rather Than Points

Outdoor Voices has taken a more experimental approach to loyalty, moving beyond point systems and levels. To start, the company offers community-wide events for customers to attend. From runs to yoga sessions, customers have access to the team and can get closer to the brand. This leads customers to be more invested and active in the brand, which likely drives sales as well.

### It Can Take Advantage of Loyalty Drivers

For too long, loyalty has been a post-transaction process, a way to get customers to come back. Smart companies are looking more broadly for loyalty drivers, for those elements in the customer journey that allow brand loyalty to be tapped and strengthened. Forrester Research found ways mobile could engage customers in loyalty building throughout the shopping life cycle including rewarding non-purchase activities such as browsing and asking questions, using past purchase and location data to make recommendations, and offering content that helps customers enjoy their new purchases[11].

This research helps reveal the vast opportunities in mobile loyalty marketing. By sticking to the plastic card, retailers ignore the opportunities mobile opens to engage customers and reward them, over and over, for their loyalty to the brand.

### It Can Make the Transaction Itself a Loyalty Driver

When is paying the bill a loyalty driver? When mobile technology transforms the payment process itself into a bonding moment. One way to achieve this is to use mobile technology to meld payments and relationships. This happens when brands offer customers a chance to pay via dedicated mobile apps.

When Walmart rolled out Walmart Pay, an app payment system delivered via mobile phone, here's how the company described its offering:

"Built with the goal of improving how customers check out and dramatically expanding mobile payment access, Walmart Pay is like no other mobile payments solution available today. With this launch, Walmart becomes the only retailer to offer its own payment solution that works with any iOS or Android device (that can download the Walmart mobile app), at any checkout lane, and with any major credit, debit, pre-paid or Walmart gift card – all through the Walmart mobile app."[12]

Walmart allows shoppers to shop without cards – without wallets! – and to simply cruise into stores and wave their phones at checkout.

Bank of America moved its loyalty program mobile when it introduced the ability to redeem rewards for BankAmericard Cash Rewards and BankAmericard Travel Rewards credit cards. Customers can easily view their available rewards or travel purchase points and redeem their desired amount through the app. The act of payment thus becomes an opportunity to inspire and reward loyalty.

## *Mobile Payment Is a Loyalty Opportunity*

Mobile payments are far from new. Credit and debit cards have been tied to mobile devices and used in card-free transactions for more than a decade now, but they still account for an almost negligible percentage of all payment transactions. Why have consumers been so slow to adopt this new technology? As is often the case with new payment technologies, there's a chicken-and-egg battle going on to convince both consumers and retailers to adopt the new methods.

People might disagree about just how much more convenient it is to pay with a phone versus a plastic card, but there's no debating that mobile payments are more secure than their traditional "card swipe" counterparts. There are two factors to this enhanced security. First, every transaction can easily be made to require a pin code or thumbprint. Second, the major mobile payment providers like Apple, Google, and Samsung all use tokenization to ensure the card number isn't stored on either the consumer's phone or the retailer's POS terminal.

One other critical factor that cannot be ignored is the rising tide of smartphone usage in our daily lives. Many consumers today are always within two feet of their mobile devices. Virtually every aspect of their daily lives is augmented in some way by these devices, and there's no sign this trend is slowing down. If mobile payments are convenient, safe, and available from a critical mass of retailers, a shift toward them is inevitable. As this happens, connecting loyalty to payment methods is a big opportunity for forward-thinking brands.

Starbucks, for example, includes mobile payment in its mobile loyalty efforts. It allows customers to use its app to preorder drinks and arrive at the store to pick up the freshly prepared product. Why wait until after the transaction to establish loyalty? Starbucks makes its pitch to customers up front: be loyal to us, and we'll save you the wait in line at the coffee shop.

What's more, the Starbucks app allows customers to load money onto their mobile accounts, track their rewards, and use them directly from their phones at checkout. It's an immediate delivery for displayed loyalty.

This is smart thinking for a company like Starbucks, which can't count on loyalty to last without constant care. The coffee business is a competitive one, with opportunities for customers to buy on virtually every street corner. Starbucks uses loyalty concepts to keep customers from straying to rivals such as Dunkin' Donuts.

Points are nice, but if you're waiting for your customer to buy a Venti double-shot mocha Frappuccino before you say thank you, you might find you've been left for another coffee purveyor. The lesson: think loyalty early and often.

## *"Mobile Minutes" Are Loyalty Opportunities*

Another important loyalty trend revolves around apps, not native apps, but the other ones on which users spend so much of their mobile time. Facebook, Instagram, Snapchat – these are the apps your customers use to run their mobile social lives.

What if you could "borrow" some of these mobile minutes? That's the tactic some smart brands are exploring to expand their loyalty marketing into the mobile space. While many brands have considered loyalty marketing that takes place in a brand-only space, others are learning these loyalty moments can be crafted onto third-party social platforms such as Facebook and Instagram. Given where many mobile customers spend so much of their time, this makes perfect sense.

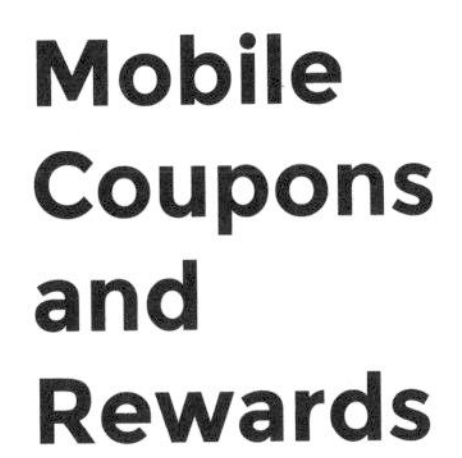

Here's how Michael Kors handles borrowed moments for loyalty marketing. In a previous incarnation, Michael Kors used Instagram to mine for email addresses. Customers were asked to sign in using an email address, and every time a customer "liked" an Instagram picture on the platform, a link to a nearby store was emailed to the customer. Nothing wrong with that, but it hardly inspired loyalty, let alone love.

Then Michael Kors relaunched its Instagram, called InstaKors, with loyalty in mind. For customers who regularly engaged with the brand via InstaKors, the company offered special promotions. Once a year, it offered special early access to view and shop for new products in the Michael Kors line. Far from seeing this as a pitch tool, Michael Kors reimagined Instagram as a way to foster a social loyalty program. It did not own this space; it "borrowed" it to create an experience in which most loyal mobile users could feel connected to both community and rewards[13].

The expansion of loyalty marketing to the mobile world won't be that hard. The truth is, customers are already prepped for it. In its research, Forrester found that 54% of consumers want mobile coupons and rewards but that only 40% of companies are testing or using mobile to deliver loyalty rewards[14].

## *Prepare to Travel from Loyalty to Obsession*

Attention to mobile loyalty marketing serves an even greater purpose in larger organizations. It leads brands closer to what Forrester calls "customer obsession," the platform that will determine success in retail engagement in the decades ahead[15].

# Forces behind the Evolution of Retail

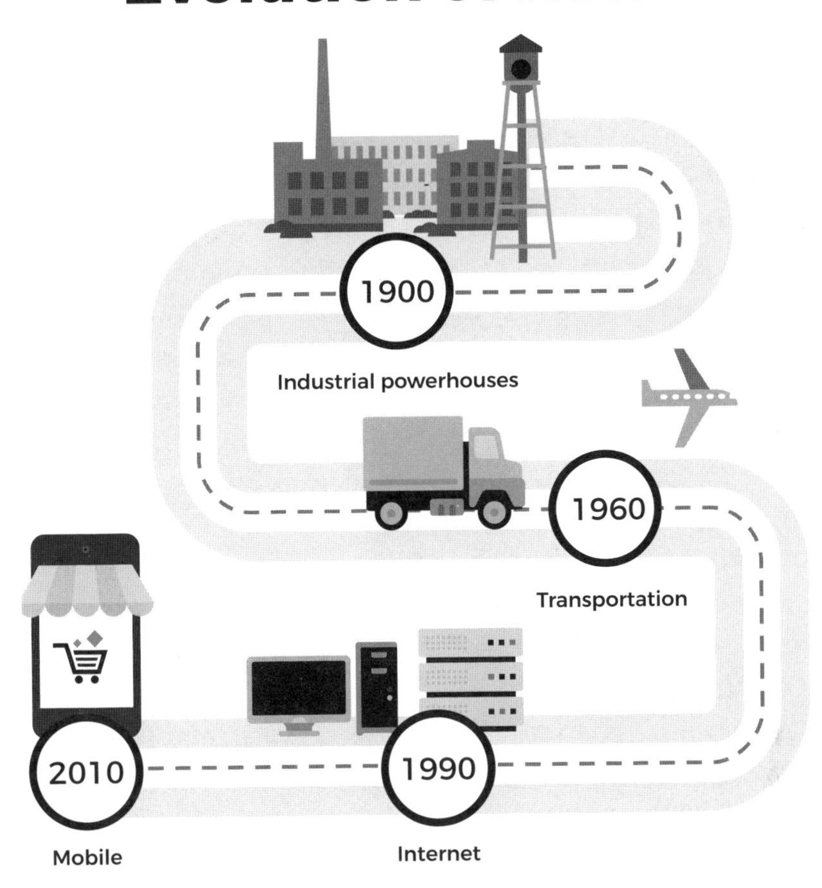


If you look back at the history of business, cycles of change are evident. In 1900, huge leaps in manufacturing produced industrial powerhouse companies. In the 1960s, advances such as global transportation systems allowed successful companies to capitalize on distribution. In the early 1990s, with the advent of the internet, we entered the age of information as connected computers began to power information all over the world with lightning speed. The next phase we'll see – one Forrester says we're already in – is the age of the customer[16].

This is more than just the usual lip service brands give to focusing on customers. The age of the customer is one in which the customer is in true control, able to access brands at any time, under a variety of circumstances. It's also one in which customers can just as easily turn off notifications or even uninstall apps at will. This creates a state of increased competition between brands on devices. Constant innovation is critical disruption, and competition can happen at any moment. Brands must battle all the time to keep customers in the fold. This focus on loyalty will be a core element of the customer obsession process.

Loyal customers are waiting. And to pass the time, they're gazing into the screens on their smartphones.

## *To Wrap Up:*

- Traditional loyalty cards are dead. They represent an old way of thinking about loyalty – let customers build points and hope they'll never use them. A loyalty program that relies on colored plastic is hopelessly behind mobile-enabled shoppers. These programs were highly successful for many years, but customer expectations are higher today. Thanks to Passbook and Apple Wallet, you can now also have virtual cards on smartphones without needing to install an app. These virtual cards can be used for payment check-in and much more. They can be updated automatically and are location and time aware. What's more, smart companies are building on the old loyalty points system, turning to experiences and opportunities as rewards for loyalty.

- Mobile opens a loyalty dialogue. Now the true driver of loyalty is not just a gift of points but a chance to engage and provide real value. Armed with mobile technology, store associates can communicate with customers and determine which reward to offer and when, providing a personalized loyalty experience.

- From loyalty to love to obsession. While current technology allows brands to move from loyalty to love, mobile will expand so that customers will come to expect more – to the level of obsession. As customers become more accustomed to personalized loyalty rewards, they will expect brands to stay engaged and focused on their wants and needs.

## *Next Steps:*

- Make your loyalty program a mobile experience. The days of plastic cards are over. With customers fully loyal to their phones, it makes sense to connect loyalty programs to customers' most prized possessions. If you insist your customers display loyalty by carrying a plastic card or calling an 800 number, you might find you are disappointed with their decision to cling to their phones rather than your brand.

- Review your existing customer journey across touch points and find opportunities to reward loyalty.

- Engage in loyalty marketing as an ongoing dialogue with customers, not just a post-purchase reward. With phones in hand, customers are presenting brands with multiple opportunities to offer rewards. Don't let these opportunities pass you by.
- Plan to move from loyalty to love to customer obsession. Cultivate your customer relationships through dedicated programs that elevate their loyalty. Just as we've seen retail transition over the decades through the age of manufacturing, distribution, and information, the time period we're in now is the age of the customer. Customer obsession will be the winning attitude.

## Voices from the Mobile Makeover

*Casey Antonelli, Director of Corporate Communications, NewStore*

All Casey wanted was a sweater. What she got was a lesson in how ready shoppers and associates are for mobile — and how far some brands are from offering it in a meaningful way.

On a business trip in a major city, Casey awoke to much colder temperatures than expected, so she ducked into a department store near the convention she was attending.

The sales associate who helped her couldn't have been nicer, but she didn't know a thing about Casey. Despite the fact that Casey was a loyal shopper at this store in her home city, this away team didn't have any background on her. Still, Casey was able to find the sweater she needed and a few other items. At the sales associate's request, she left her cell phone number and headed back to her work event.

The next day, Casey received a text. And then another. The sales associate had hunted down two other items she thought Casey might like.

The thought was there, but the technology was not. Instead of having a feature-rich dedicated app, the store associate was working with the basics of her own personal smartphone. The photographs of the two items were poor — they were laid out on a white counter, in meager light. Casey couldn't figure out if they looked attractive or not. She didn't get any product information or pricing.

Casey sighed. She was ready to be a loyal customer, and the sales associate was ready to go the extra mile to make her happy, but the technology in between wasn't up to the job.

Loyalty, squandered.

# Chapter 5

# The Corporate Relationship Makeover

**Insights**

- Silos in your organization can kill your mobile makeover before it starts.
- A new breed of retail leadership is rising up via ecommerce.

**Location:** Corporate Headquarters

**Time:** Today

In the conference room, the regulars have taken their seats. On one side of the table, the VP of Retail and her underlings are set, armed with binders stacked in front of them like a rampart. On the other side of the table, the VP of Ecommerce and his team are also prepared, laptops open, Excel running, data at the ready. Toward the front of the room, the representative from IT has taken her position. At precisely 9:00 a.m., the glass doors swing open and the CEO enters, assistant in tow, and takes his seat at the head of the long polished oak table.

The CEO surveys the scene. He feels a strong sense of déjà vu, as though he's been in this meeting before. He's hopeful this time will be different.

The CEO sits back as the meeting begins and his executives spar over the challenges created by new technology. He's spent decades in this company, starting as a sales associate, then moving up through the ranks of operations to now occupy the corner office. And, yes, he's been in this meeting before. Many times before, hearing the same arguments from the same players. There's still no resolution, no clear path forward to reconcile the nature of his retail operation in a marketplace where mobile has flipped the shopping cart.

It's not often that anyone can muster pity for the CEOs of the world, but when it comes to handling the transformation of traditional retailers in the mobile age, it's easier to spare a bit of sympathy. Theirs is a difficult job. Many of the most successful retailers are institutions that have grown up over the decades from corner stores to beloved local institutions to national and even internationally recognized industry leaders. They are businesses of pride and tradition, and in many ways they are imbedded in the lives of their customers, where they occupy ingrained habits and fond memories.

Still, there's no question that the venerable traditional retailer is under fire in this changing world. Technology is flipping much of what made these retailers great. The human touch of high-quality customer service and the look and feel of grand physical locations are all under attack by technology that can be faster and more efficient than the most practiced salesman and just as beautiful as the most vaunted architecture. Lured by speed, low prices, and rich visuals, customer loyalty toward once-cherished retailers is wavering. Can the industry adapt and survive, or are we witnessing the end of an era?

## ***Retailers Want to Go Mobile***

The leadership of traditional retail is aware of the change that has swept the industry. Leadership is even willing to adapt. The problem is how. Many traditional retailers accept the "why" of transformation in the mobile age, but they struggle mightily with the "how." What needs to happen so this transformation can take place without bogging down in endless conference room debates over money and power?

The answer, I've found, is that traditional retailers – both cherished department stores and famous nationa l chains – need to stop skipping crucial steps when it comes to mobile transformation. By leaping to choose and execute new technology, they leave out critical changes that must take place before the tech decisions are made and the process is rolled out. To be successful in the mobile era, retail must not only transform its use of technology but also alter the human aspect of the organization. The first step is transforming the retail workforce, starting with the CEO and working through the company.

## ***The Successful Retail Organization Is Omnichannel***

Omnichannel is more than a buzzword. It's a description of what has happened to retail customers and what must happen inside the retail organization if it is to transform successfully.

Consider the way mobile-savvy customers now shop. They might power up an app when riding the train into work and see some of the new looks for summer. They might receive recommendations based on their personal taste, since they've opted in and shared their preferences on previous shopping occasions. As they browse, they might receive personalized discount offers via the app that make them think more seriously about making a purchase.

Later that day, while taking a break at work, they might browse the retailer's site on their desktops. On these larger screens, they might linger more on visuals such as the slideshow and video of the new product arrivals. Perhaps they click on the comments section to see what others have to say or toggle over to a pure play ecommerce retailer to see if their wares are similar or better priced.

After work, with a little time to kill, they might stop into the store near the office, where beacon technology alerts the sales staff and secures their browsing history from the website and mobile app visits earlier in the day. There, sales associates greet them by name, offer to start dressing rooms with the items they've viewed, and offer suggestions about other items they might like as accessories.

From a traditional retailer perspective, our shoppers have touched three "channels" of the retail business: the mobile app, the website, and the store. This channel concept is deeply embedded in retailing history. It's how retailers have organized themselves for decades. As retailers built businesses over the years, the mandate to avoid "channel conflict" was always present. There was no growth if all you were doing was stealing from one channel to fill another. Channel boundaries were to be clear and respected. This was a retail rule.

But our fictional shoppers have a very different view of the experience. While they might have technically toggled between channels, this isn't something they perceive as important or relevant. In fact, as far as they're concerned, they're shopping at their retailer. Period. Whether they're shopping via mobile app or website or store isn't relevant; to them, it's all the same thing. If these shoppers were to arrive in the store with their mobile app discount offers and be told these offers weren't "good" in the store, they'd be shocked and appalled.

## *Channel Boundaries Have Blurred*

A previous generation might have been more comfortable with the idea of separate channels. Catalogs, they knew, were a separate business from stores. One did not mix with the other. But modern shoppers aren't that forgiving. The retailer is the retailer, no matter the platform. Excuses about channels don't fly with fluid shoppers.

We call the word for the experience our shoppers desire "omnichannel." The omnichannel commerce story isn't brand new. For years, buyers have expected a consistent experience across channels. They should be able to enjoy the same experience regardless of the channels they use. However, the omnichannel story is evolving – it's now about creating an experience that mimics the way people move about the world and live.

Shoppers do not visit separate commerce channels independently. They are in a position to engage multiple channels simultaneously, in particular the mobile channel in combination with others. The omnichannel imperative stems from the idea that retailers and shoppers are in constant, uninterrupted communication across platforms. This is more extensive than "multichannel," which simply suggests that multiple options exist for shoppers. "Omnichannel" conveys a vision of always on, always fluid, always with shoppers, no matter what device or format they opt to use.

Some companies are already showing omnichannel leadership. Nordstrom, for example, demonstrates this in its simplified conversion process. Customers on Nordstrom's Instagram feed can instantly buy the merchandise they see there. The Nordstrom app provides digital versions of the retail catalogs. At Nordstrom, marketing, sales, and retail operations work together to ensure a seamless customer experience.

Apple is also known for its omnichannel execution. The company has integrated online and offline shopping for years. If you're interested in an Apple Watch, you can look at the various models on your desktop, set up a time to meet with an Apple concierge to try on in the store, and when you're ready, order a customer model online from inside the store or make your purchase with a store associate. An Apple employee can check you out wherever you are in the store using an iPhone as a register. Omnichannel makes perfect sense to shoppers but flies in the face of the organizational structure retailers have used for decades.

## *Bring Down the Silos*

Let's go back to our story about the CEO and his morning meeting. What's happening in that meeting is an obvious case of channel conflict. The VP of Retail is defending her turf. She wants resources to flow to the stores, and she's not going to sit idly by while the ecommerce department siphons off money and customers from her channel. Across the table, the VP of Ecommerce is battling to have his channel achieve parity with the long-dominant retail channel. He's aware that ecommerce is often considered the interloper within the retail organization. Then we have yet another constituency, IT. Whatever the VPs come up with, it might well fall to her department to implement. Just as the other execs defend their channels, she's pushed to defend her department.

This is a classic description of silos, and it's the organizational reality that blocks retailers from achieving an omnichannel experience. If each department maintains its walls and turf defense, omnichannel is blocked. The first step in transformation for the mobile age is attacking the silo system. As long as "channels" remain, with defined walls and spheres of influence, the omnichannel shopping experience is thwarted. How to overcome this?

- Some companies are addressing the silo issue by creating a new position. "Head of Digital Experience" is one title we've seen. This person can combat channel conflict by managing digital interaction with customers no matter where they shop. That puts the head of digital in charge of ecommerce but also in charge of digital interactions that might occur in the stores, such as mobile-enabled sales associates. This takes the digital experience out of the battle zone between two VPs. With a broader mandate for all things digital, the new position crosses channel lines and begins the process of tearing down the walls between warring departments.

- Consider unifying profit and loss (P&L) statements. One of the biggest barriers to change is that the retail and ecommerce organizations have separate P&L goals. People act on incentives. With two different P&Ls, organizations will continue to be at odds.
- Another method we've seen companies use is seeking and promoting a new class of senior leadership, one that comes up through the ecommerce ranks. For many decades, the path to the corner office in a retailer ran through operations or perhaps finance, but ecommerce talent was not in on that hunt. Now, as ecommerce operations have matured, so have their executives. Those individuals are now in the running for top retail jobs. Choosing a CEO with an ecommerce background is another way to bring the omnichannel experience into reality and infuse digital DNA into the entire organization. Often, these are the executives with hands-on experience with new technologies. They understand how technology-enabled shopping fits into the broader retail experience.

## *Transformation Is Happening — Across Departments*

Along with the CEO who has an ecommerce background, other new types of retail employees are on the rise to meet the omnichannel challenge. Experimenting with new mobile technologies and platforms might come naturally to many consumers, but can the same be said for senior level executives and marketing decision makers? Perhaps not as readily. However, it's happening at other levels of the organizational chart as indicated below:

- Marketing. First, mobile is transforming the lowest tier of marketing within organizations and paving the way for a slew of new jobs such as social media account executives and directors who are tasked with being the face of the brand and connecting directly with consumers. Mobile allows news and buzz-worthy moments to go viral in an instant. This means brands must continuously leverage social media to participate in ongoing conversations and quell damaging feedback. After all, no company can afford to ignore a negative setback of any sort that prompts a storm of angry tweets. One of the best examples of prime low-tier mobile marketing can be found among airlines. These companies are frequently inundated with frustrated travelers' complaints or requests, spurring them to staff their social media accounts with round-the-clock support that individually answers each comment. A missed comment is a missed marketing opportunity. Mobile also influences the upper marketing echelons of every organization by turning senior level executives' attention toward programmatic buying. Brands' programmatic spend is projected to double in the next several years, meaning that CEOs, CMOs, and other organization leaders will be forced to decide exactly how much of their advertising budgets they're willing to allocate toward mobile. Mobile's ability to help marketers more effectively target audiences by demographics lends credence to higher allocations; however, this will depend on the amount of education surrounding mobile marketing that executives receive.

- Customer service. Additionally, mobile continues to make its way up the marketing ladder by transforming how customer service issues are handled. Marketers such as Hyatt are tapping Facebook Messenger as a direct line leading to customers, enabling them to speak to a brand representative through one of their most used mobile messaging platforms.
- IT. New skills are needed today to develop and maintain complex IT stacks powering omnichannel operations. Brand-new tech talent is needed to develop and maintain brands' mobile presence across iOS, Android, and mobile web.
- Store operations. Retailers must work closely with their ecommerce teams to attract digitally savvy store associates.

As we see these changes occur throughout the organization, they offer a pathway for the company as a whole. Mobile is steadily and deftly transforming internal management within companies by creating new positions, opening up new avenues of bridging two-way conversations with customers, and providing incentives for additional education concerning digital platforms. It's up to all company employees to push mobile strategies and initiatives through their organizations until they land on the desks of CMOs and CEOs. If this does not happen, internal management might become stagnant in its use of revenue-making tools and lose out on the loyalty of a very sought-after demographic of consumers: mobile-minded millennials.

## *Omnichannel Requires New HR Policies*

Transforming the organization for the mobile age also requires a look at policies. Some of the most pressing involve compensation.

Many sales associates work on commission. This has long been the process designed to inspire them to top-notch customer service, but the mobile era upsets this process. If the customer engages with a mobile sales rep via the app but buys in the store, who banks the sale? If the customer is helped in the store but then goes home and purchases via the website, who gets paid? If the customer toggles frequently between all the different platforms available, who gets credited with the rise in sales activity? The technology blurs the lines and makes it harder for employers to understand who is making an impact. It can also stir controversy among staffers, leaving them wondering if their commissions are at risk.

Other compensation issues revolve around hours worked. Suppose a store associate works his shift and then clocks out for the day but receives a text message from a customer that evening. Naturally, he will want to take care of his best customer as he's been trained to do. But if he answers the text, how many hours has he worked, and are these hours overtime?

These are not small considerations for a large retail organization. The way in which associates are compensated must be transparent to all in order to serve as a motivational tool.

When associates are confused, they might hold back, unsure of whether their efforts will be rewarded.

While the answers to these questions are complicated, I believe the first step is not less involvement with technology but more. The more the mobile device is attached to the sales associate's hand, the more the employer will be able to understand, through the data collected, what's happening and when. It is through the transformation to the mobile age that retailers will be able to track and evaluate the contribution of each salesperson.

## *Prepare for Scalability*

Retailers also struggle to manage mobile-related growth. Most retailers dream of continuous and consistent growth. From the world's largest chains to a single mom-and-pop operation, a steady increase in clientele helps ward off the dangers of lean times and makes cash flow forecasting and inventory ordering easier, but growth can come at a cost. If demand exceeds supply, you can quickly see your reputation become damaged as frustrated customers voice their thoughts online.

This has happened more than once when companies have taken on new marketing or advertising campaigns that caught on faster than expected. Perhaps, as in one particular case, a celebrity is hired as a spokesperson. This individual's popularity generates a sharp spike in customer visits to a retailer's website, but the servers can't handle the load and the site crashes. The anticipation and enjoyment the prospective customers felt are replaced with frustration and anger that sometimes can't be rectified. Often, the damage is done, a reputation is destroyed, and at least some of those shoppers jump to the competition.

The statistics on site abandonment are shocking. It takes only a fraction of a second for people to grow disinterested and move elsewhere, even when everything works fine. This can translate into thousands or even millions of dollars of lost revenue, either immediately during the delay or over the longer term.

Scalability is not easy. To survive the onslaught of a spike in demand, a retailer's website must be scalable. It must be able to grow in a fraction of a second in the case of a reaction to an ad campaign. It must also be able to handle the slower, larger-scale expansion brought on by the adoption of a new channel like a mobile ecommerce site, an app, or a new payment or search system.

This is one of those situations that requires management and IT to be on the same page and in the same room. Very often, a retailer's IT department is overloaded and stretched between too many other projects. At other times, it might only exist as an extension of the marketing department. Budget and resource concerns can easily overrule any proactive initiatives. IT and management might not even speak the same language in the sense that one talks in broad concepts and the other talks in computerese.

The solution is for management to recognize that successful omnichannel commerce relies on keeping a close eye on platform scalability. Given the permanently valid knowledge that an ounce of prevention is worth a pound of cure, management must recognize that the cost of an outage far exceeds the cost of building and maintaining a scalable platform.

This demands the creation and coordination of a reliable team internally and possibly also using external consultants and experts. It also requires that the two sides, management and IT, learn to talk to each other in a mutually comprehensible way. On the surface, retail is about brands, fashions, and products, but none of that will happen if a stable and scalable system isn't running behind the scenes to process orders and payments, show off merchandise on smartphones, tablets, and PC screens, and ensure that last-mile delivery is completed.

The worlds of IT, marketing, and retail are colliding. The result is a new frontier of business growth, but only for those who are willing to invest in an ounce of prevention.

## *Is Your Organization Ready?*

Can you meet the questions in the conference room with confidence and reason? Here's a cheat sheet of responses to help you debunk 12 common superstitions that dog modern mobile commerce.

It's natural to fear change, and fear is the root of superstition, but change is inevitable. Mobile will continue to grow dramatically as the omnipotent force of commerce. Is your organization prepped to change with the times or resigned to retiring to the history books?

Yesterday 14:44

Mobile commerce is a money pit.

Actually, it makes money – a ton of money for many. Customers use your native mobile app when they want deep engagement with you. This leads to far greater conversion and loyalty than websites or mobile sites.

It's too complicated 

That is why retailers must collaborate with people who know about technology in retail. Just like choosing great suppliers and advertising people – let the experts help you!

Mobile is not secure enough 

Given the rise in credit card fraud, mobile payment technology – especially single-click options like Apple Pay or Android Pay – is much safer.

This is not how retail does things.

Sure, but you could say the same about debit cards, cash registers, barcodes, and SKUs. Every new thing starts somewhere, and you can be an innovator! 🙂

It's too risky 

You should probably not go into the retail business if you are not willing to face some risk. In business as in life, there is no such thing as standing still. Find out what the risks are, and then do what needs to be done to handle them.

**Read** Yesterday

**Today** 9:44

Mobile is not profitable 

Mobile has a huge influence on a consumer's purchasing decision: around 80 percent. Mobile-first purchases as a percentage of mobile commerce are projected to be $800 billion annually by 2018.

**Delivered**

Today 10:12

Online is not as important as in-store.

Not true 😬 $1.3 trillion of retail is influenced by mobile. Retailers often keep digital commerce as its own division with a separate P&L, which further segregates it. Suggestion: Do not ever say "ecommerce." Take the "e" away. It is all commerce, and should be blended accordingly.

A mobile site is just a desktop made smaller.

When a retailer simply reproduces its desktop website on a phone screen, it throws away opportunities for mobile customer engagement 😟 Mobile is its own thing and connects more intimately to the shopper.

The customer base is too diverse 😎

Yes, it may be diverse. But, they all have the Internet in common. It is up to you to target customers individually. Technology does this for you.

We already rely on Black Friday and Christmas.

Seasonal events are still significant, but there is more that can be done year-round. A real-time world does not exclusively use calendar milestones for every shopping need.

Our competitors are not using this 🙄

If you know this for certain, then you will have an edge by going mobile. The odds are they either have it or are working on it. If your CURRENT competitors have not gone mobile, beware – your next NEW competitor might launch with a mobile-first strategy and eat your lunch.

Our customers don't want this.

It is more likely they either do not know you offer mobile, or they are discovering that you don't 😉 They will probably drift to other sellers pretty soon, who satisfy their demand for the mobile experience.

Delivered

## ***To Wrap Up:***

- Your silos are killing you. Until you break down those walls, you will never catch the mobile wave. If your company treats mobile like a project within the ecommerce department, it will be blocked from fulfilling its true potential as a way to improve sales across the company.
- Consider building an organization that's channel agnostic. Customers aren't thinking about moving from one channel to another; they simply want to access your store anywhere, anytime, on any device. Adopt their unified vision and don't sort your touch points into channels.
- Plan for a scalable future. Perhaps the greatest disappointment to a customer is a service that works well for a while and then flounders. Plan for success by envisioning a company that's fully mobile and omnichannel by planning for scalable technology early on.

## *Next Steps:*

- Hunt honestly for your silos. What walls divide your organization? These are the walls that must come down for omnichannel to become a reality. Is the division between retail and ecommerce? Between managers and associates? Where are divisions cropping up, and what can you do to make connections?
- Consider hiring a VP of Digital. This isn't another layer of management; it's a way to unite the digital experience for the company and customer.
- Consider unifying P&L rather than allowing retail and digital to operate separately. Only when incentives are unified will the two groups be able to work in concert. With separate P&L, they remain at odds.
- Tap the full organization to test, learn, and teach mobile technology. You might find your best mobile insights come from your employees – at all levels of the organization – using and evaluating mobile efforts. Don't assume the testing process must be walled off in a lab. Your new marketing junior associate might uncover insights you never imagined.

## Voices from the Mobile Makeover

*Martijn Cornelissen, Chief Digital Officer, Leapp*
*(former Head of Global Commerce at Rituals)*

For Rituals, the move to mobile started close to home. "When we created our new head office, we decided we would have only mobile phones in the office, no old-fashioned telephones, so that was forward-thinking," says Martijn Cornelissen.

This decision led the way for changes at every level of the company. Today, Rituals store managers have the ability to see store revenues on their phones on an hourly basis, and the focus going forward is on the customer experience. "If the customer wants to connect with you, you need to respond in the right way, either via chat or app," says Cornelissen. "Then, we are working to create a unified experience. When the customer wants to have contact with Rituals, they don't care if they bought online or in a store. They think Rituals needs to know their behavior and be able to help them. We're not quite there yet; we're quite siloed, but this is the goal, to close the gap and have one customer account with all the information. Over time, we will be able to use this data to better service them."

The move to mobile is merely a recognition of the obvious customer preference, says Cornelissen. "People look at their phones 200 to 250 times a day. If they reach out to Rituals, mobile is a fast and easy way to really connect. It's personal; it's preferred. Customers know they are in charge."

The biggest challenge that lies ahead? It's not technology, says Cornelissen, but people. "My biggest obstacle is not on the technology side. It's much more around building the right organization. We want to make sure everyone on the team is agile and flexible enough to move with all the changes that lie ahead. Big international brands tend to be slow. We need to have a team that is flexible, can influence management, and find the right partners."

## Chapter 6

# The Technology Relationship Makeover

**Insights**

- A retail CTO needs a broad set of skills in innovation, experimentation, and strategy.
- Partnerships, not solo efforts, offer the best outcomes for retailers as they transform for the mobile age.

In a book like this, it might be tempting to open first to this chapter – the one about technology – to see what technology is recommended in a world flipped by mobile. But the technology relationship makeover is less about technology itself and much more about the people tasked with managing it. These are the CTOs, the CIOs, and the managers who will make the technology decisions that transform their companies for the mobile age.

We know technology is changing rapidly and that this will continue. There will be new software to test, new platforms to try, new ways to use technology to reach and delight customers. This chapter is not about how your *technology* must transform. That's a given. This chapter is about how your *chief technologist* must transform. The most important makeover in technology must happen on a human scale.

## Start by Understanding the Hype Cycle

The first step in the makeover of the CTO comes in our understanding of what many observers in the technology industry call the Hype Cycle. This is a five-step process applied to many technology innovations. It rolls out like this:

1. The Technology Trigger. This is the new technology that bursts onto the scene, offering a brand-new way to do something. At this stage, the new technology garners a lot of media interest but offers up very few actual examples of its prowess in action. Is it commercially viable? Who knows?

2. Peak of Inflated Expectations. The media attention leads to a few highly touted success stories and usually a much larger group of failures. Some companies have acted on this new technology, but most have not.

3. Trough of Disillusionment. As the failures pile up, interest in the technology begins to fall off. A shakeout of the early players takes place. Some investment continues in the products embraced by early adopters.

4. Slope of Enlightenment. At this point, if we visualize the process, we turn upward out of the valley the Trough of Disillusionment created. Benefits of the technology start to emerge. Second- and third-generation

products and more funding become available. Forward-thinking companies step up while more conservative firms continue to sit on the sidelines.

5. Plateau of Productivity. This is the point at which mainstream adoption of the technology becomes a reality. Broad market appeal becomes clear, viability is more concretely assessable, and everyone gets it.

For the CTO in the retail space, it's important to understand where we are in the Hype Cycle of mobile shopping. Clearly, mobile technology overall is well adopted. We walk around with our phones in our hands and have to be reminded to look up from the screens. But the process of shopping via mobile is not at the same stage. Mobile shopping isn't entirely new but neither is it mainstream. Where are we, and why does it matter?

Looking at the behavior of shoppers and major retailers, you could argue that we're in the early period of coming out of the disillusionment phase. Looking at a graphic of the Hype Cycle, retail is just to the right of the valley – not at the bottom of viability but not at the top, either. Rather, it's just on the brink of a takeoff.

This is critical to the makeover of the retail CTO. The knowledge that mobile shopping is on the precipice of a new phase has a dramatic impact on how the CTO must behave going forward.

## The Hype Cycle of Mobile Shopping

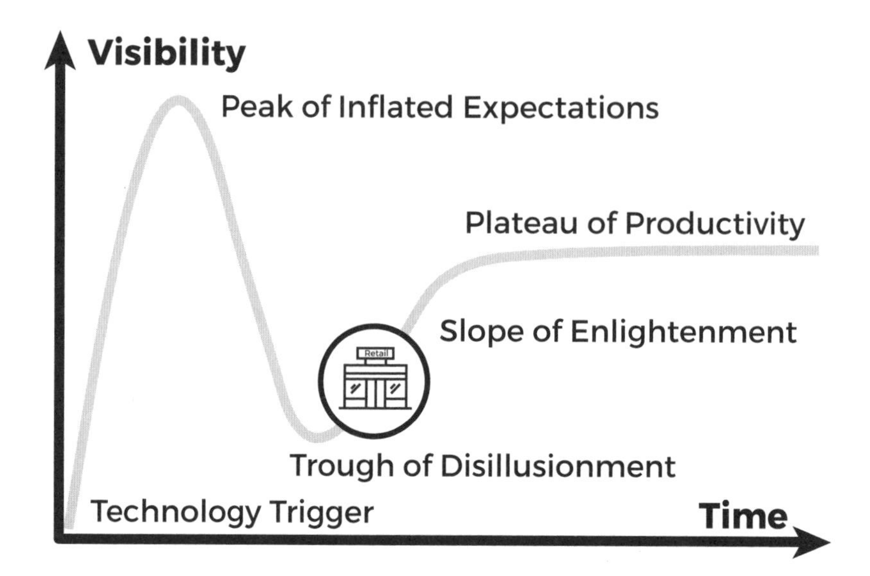


### *Managing for the Slope of Enlightenment*

To successfully lead retailers into an environment in which mobile has flipped the shopping cart, and is poised for take-off, CTOs need more than technology skills. They need to lead on three critical fronts: innovation, experimentation, and strategy.

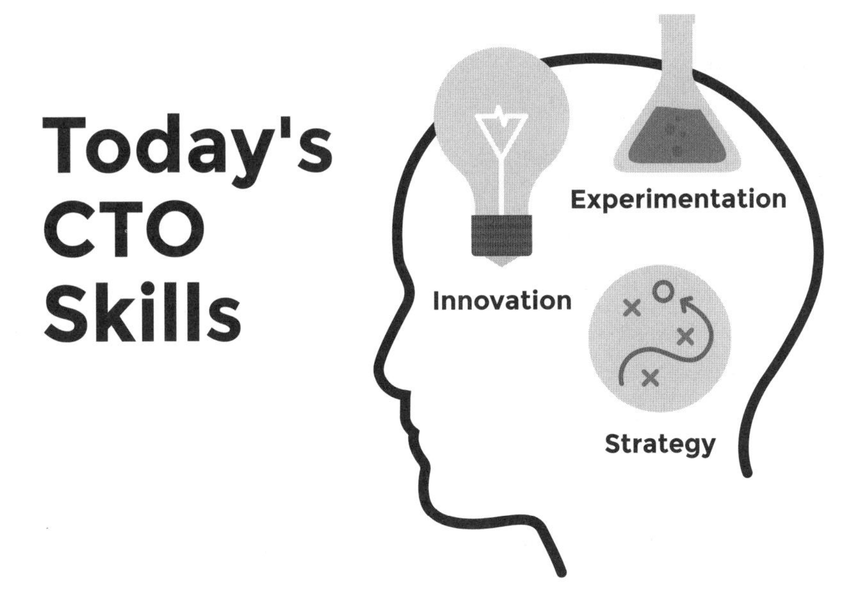


### Chief Innovator

CTOs must be the central point of innovation information for the company. This goes far beyond reviewing the latest wares at trade shows; it requires CTOs to think fundamentally about the innovation process and how it must play out in retailers for long-term success.

For one thing, CTOs must stop thinking of technology vendors as vendors.

"Vendor" is a word that works against the necessary innovation process. It's not a word that inspires deep connection and positive emotion. When you say "vendor," you're already placing a business in a subcategory, one of those annoying ones that crops up when you need to argue about a bill or debate the value of a deliverable. There's no love in a vendor relationship. Calling a business your "vendor" labels it an outsider.

This is contraindicated for the innovation process. When you want true innovation, you need partners, and this need for partnership isn't unique to retailing. Across industries, companies are realizing that great innovation is a collaborative process, one that often taps specialists from outside a firm to come in and realize the disruption that is possible.

Automakers partner with technology firms in search of autonomous cars. Healthcare seeks lower costs and streamlined delivery in partnership with technology firms. To see them as vendors – temporary service providers – is to wall off the necessary relationship that leads to innovation in any industry.

This focus on innovation partnership is often the most profitable way forward for retail CTOs. The truth is, most retailers must partner rather than attempt to go it alone on technological innovation.

The key word is "most." There will be a few well-capitalized retailers that can truly afford to make this investment, but for the vast majority of retailers and brands, that level of investment in in-house tech staff is prohibitive.

Frankly, technology talent is expensive. When non-tech industries try to create their own in-house technology labs, this is often the first hurdle they face. The best and brightest in Silicon Valley typically intend to stay there. Moving to the headquarters of a traditional company isn't a popular career path. Few retailers would be able to lure this talent away anyway, and even if they did, imagine the unrest it would cause when word spread of the salary it took to hire this talent. The in-house technology lab, while a possibility for some true giants in retailing, is financially out of reach for most of the industry.

Still, to partner with the right technologists, CTOs must look for a certain mind-set from their partners, including a willingness to walk a mile in the retailer's shoes. While retailers must learn to partner, technologists must learn to retail.

To innovate on the part of retailers, technologists must be more connected to the world in which retail takes place. The world of technology is a far cry from the sales floor. Tech experts often have little contact with the mass of humanity that walks into stores every day. CTOs seeking innovation partners should look for tech firms that are willing to put hours into walking the sales floor with an associate or shadowing a manager. Technology experts will find their own creativity sparked by working a shift as a pick-and-pack specialist at a client's warehouse. Taking the time to gain this level of on-the-job understanding is a key way innovation is fostered, and it must be a key priority of the retail CTO.

## Chief Experimenter

When Nordstrom hired a Chief Technology Officer, it looked for more than just a history of tech knowledge; it recruited specifically for an individual with a successful history of experimenting.

Experimentation will be a vital tool in the transformation of retail for the mobile age. It will be the way CTOs turn their hunches into smart actions. Nordstrom is hardly the only retailer following this path. Walmart acquired Jet.com to access the start-up's innovation and experimentation talent. Then Walmart tested its own mobile app payment system in a selection of stores before rolling it out nationwide. Retailers such as Staples and Home Depot have created innovation labs to test and tweak technology. The ability to create, run, and learn from experimentation is a key skill for the retail CTO, one that will only become more critical as new technologies emerge and shoppers look for new ways to engage with their favorite brands.

Experiments are already in progress throughout the industry. Neiman Marcus is trying out a virtual reality memory mirror, actually a giant video screen and camera, that enables shoppers to see outfits from 360 degrees and compare clothing options side by side. It also remembers what customers have already tried on. Meanwhile, Japanese retailer Rakuten is testing drone delivery to consumers. In the U.K., companies like Just Eat are testing droids as delivery vehicles. Retailers using Deliv and other ridesharing services for delivery are investigating the possibility of using driverless cars. These companies all share the need for smart experimentation.

Individual technologies such as these might ultimately catch fire or they might wither, but they've already succeeded in demonstrating a new dimension of in-person shopping: providing a convenience and magic that have faded from the retail shop floor. Retailers shouldn't shy away from experiments like these. They are not gimmicks; they are the process of innovation at work.

### Chief Strategist

Finally, it will fall to the CTO to craft a plan forward. Identifying the right technology is necessary, and understanding how that technology will fit into the business is critical, but all that will fall flat unless the CTO can lead the organization forward into the right decision, into the upward slope of enlightenment that is starting to emerge in the mobile shopping industry.

Retail CTOs prepared to mesh company goals with mobile possibilities must take several steps.

## *Steps to Mesh Company Goals with Mobile Possibilities*

### Step One: Assess the Company's Strategic Goals

What are your strategic goals for the short, medium, and long term? The list might be long and varied or it might focus on a few key areas. It could include any of the following:

- Improving consumer engagement. Smart retailers know the key to sales is engagement, an ongoing conversation between retailer and shopper that leads to loyalty, conversions, and repeat visits. Are you looking at ways to improve engagement, to keep customers in the store longer or to engage with them outside the four walls of your store in a way that's meaningful and relevant to them? Are you looking for ways to make connections that result in powerful long-term relationships?

- Gaining a better understanding of customers. Do you wish you knew more about what customers want at any given time? Do you wonder what they're thinking when they walk into the store? Do you wish you had a window into what makes them happy and what leaves them cold?

- Observing and analyzing customer behavior. Where do your customers go when they enter the store?

Where do they walk? What do they look at? What paths do they travel and why?

- Making payments as simple as possible. Have you ever lost a sale due to a long line at the checkout counter? Do you worry that your virtual abandoned shopping carts on your ecommerce site are due to payment hiccups? Do you wish you could make the payment process faster and less cumbersome?
- Enabling an endless aisle concept. Do you envision a day when your sales associate never has to look at a customer and say, "Sorry, we don't have that item in stock. Maybe try our other location?" Can you see a bonus in giving that sales associate full chain-wide inventory visibility to serve the customer right then and there?
- Delivering goods as quickly as possible. Do you wish your products could get to your customer with all the speed of the average pizza? Do you know your customer would appreciate more options when it comes to delivery? Do you see the disruption in the traditional fulfillment process and wonder how that could work to your advantage in your relationship with your customers?

If your strategic goals are to be faster, more targeted, and in closer touch with your customer, mobile is ready for you.

In-store Wi-Fi is perhaps the most essential first step. Increasingly, the public sees internet access as an essential component of shopping, enabling price comparisons and product research and contributing to a positive experience. Stores that offer Wi-Fi stand to capitalize on messages delivered to customers through the website/splash/welcome screen as well as data collected through tracking and interaction. Not offering Wi-Fi might lead to reduced sales, decreased loyalty, and a lack of engagement in store.

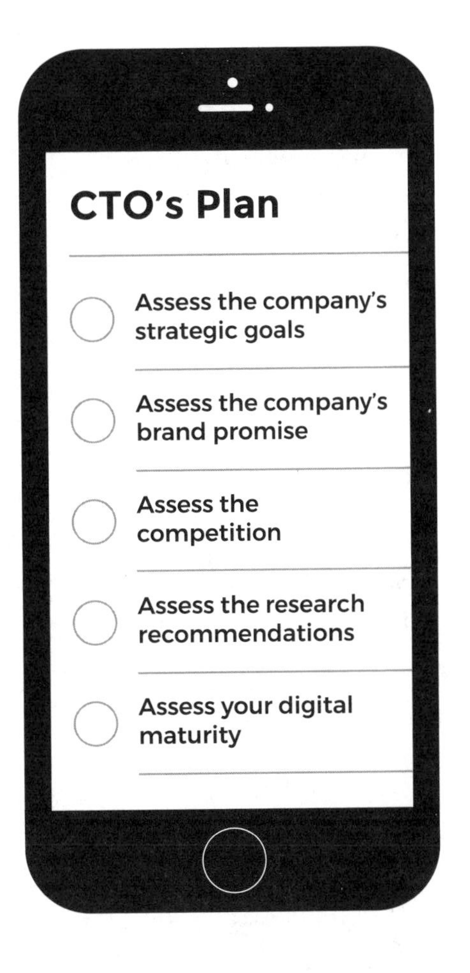


Other available tools can also get you closer to your goals. Beacon technology can tell you when a customer enters a store. It can be used to deliver personalized marketing messages to that customer. It can even detect when your customer might be passing your window display, lingering, trying to decide whether or not to enter. Beacon technology is an opt-in process, so no tracking happens without a customer's approval. Along those lines, many shoppers say they would welcome the opportunity to have more relevant offers delivered to them.

What all these ideas share is a mobile platform. Whether your goal is to understand your customers' movements, thoughts, habits, or needs, mobile is the way customers are becoming accustomed to communicating. When retailers want to reach out, customers are already holding the device they prefer.

### Step Two: Assess the Company's Brand Promise

Beyond your strategic goals, look at the promise your brand offers. What is your role in the retail landscape? Why should any shopper choose you over the many other options available in the marketplace today? This is your promise. It's part of the decision-making process consumers make on any given day. When considering mobile technology, an essential assessment technique is to examine the store's brand promise and then locate the technology that works.

When Gallup released its report "Why Your Mobile App Could Fail," the issue of brand promise played a key role. "If your mobile storefront is disconnected from your brand or brand promise, you'll not only miss out on mobile sales, you also could alienate customers from making future purchases in store or online," it warned[17].

In considering a technology investment, it pays to question both customers and employees on the topic of brand promise. Do they know what your brand represents? What are the experiences that are completely unique to your business that most engage customers? How can those experiences be conveyed on a smartphone?

Then, with a clarified vision of your brand promise, you can work to marry it with mobile technology. If the brand promise is "We have everything!" and the primary strategic objective is to enable "endless aisle," retailers should expand their technology into the back office, using RFID to improve integration of inventory into their back-end system. If the promise is to be cutting edge in regard to engaging consumers, retailers should invest in details that will augment interactions between people. If the brand promise is about delivering the product as fast as possible, the focus should turn to fulfillment technology that will facilitate this.

For retailers, brand promise must also embrace store promise – the experience customers expect when they walk into your physical store. If your store promises an attentive, knowledgeable associate who is armed and able to give the best possible service, customers will walk through the door with high expectations. That might mean looking at a series of human resources processes and examining how mobile affects them. Consider the following:

- Clarifying management principles and day-to-day operations to fulfill the promise of serving customers.
- Strategizing how clear, real-time inventory knowledge can lead to cross-sell/up-sell opportunities.
- Formulating a policy about how to incentivize employees to engage with consumers and offer advice.
- Establishing ecosystem partners in areas such as payment processing, delivery, in-store analytics, and customer care and curating this ecosystem to connect best with the target consumer, e.g., millennials.

- Staying aware of current trends and future possibilities and planning ahead. No business likes to see innovation or opportunity pass it by. For example, part of the retail fulfillment policy must be a commitment to staying up to date on innovative fulfillment methods, which requires research and awareness both through trade channels and media.

When you understand your goals, what you promise as a brand, and what your stores promise as an experience, technology choices are clarified.

### Step Three: Assess the Competition

After all that internal soul searching, your next step is to look around. What is your competition up to in the technology space?

Don't be put off by the concern that your competition is already using more advanced technology. First-mover advantage might have some benefits, but it's no reason to back away. Use your competition to see the possibilities. Look at companies that might not be your direct competitors but that are using technology in new and interesting ways. You might find these applicable to your store.

In its report identifying global "genius" brands, research firm L2 noted that leading brands are often the most inventive, pushing the confines of conventional wisdom and using technology in brave new ways. For example, it notes that even though beer doesn't have a robust ecommerce history, AB InBev launched the Bud Light Button that allows consumers to order beer with a single tap on their mobile phones.

One company's minor experiment might be another's future growth driver.

### Step Four: Assess the Research Recommendations

Research firms provide a wealth of information for retailers making technology decisions. Among the most common recommendations: technology should differentiate your company. As retailers look for ways to stand out in a crowd, technology increasingly provides that option. Shopper loyalty is often fleeting. "The next big thing" might beckon your customers, but technology can provide the edge that keeps them in the fold.

You need a CMO + CIO + Head of Retail master plan for technology. Far too often, existing silos block necessary collaboration within a company. A technology makeover such as a move to a mobile-first strategy is one that requires the input of multiple departments and consistent leadership from the highest levels. To achieve that degree of harmony, consider creating a technology master plan, one that is owned by the CMO, CIO, and the Head of Retail. Look into adding the role of CDO (Chief Digital Officer) as a way to build a management bridge across departments.

### Step Five: Assess Your Digital Maturity

Is your company ready for a digital makeover? The best plans will stall out if the company isn't ready to engage. Consider an assessment of your mobile readiness.

### Mobile Readiness Assessment for Brands

This assessment covers topics necessary for a successful rollout of mobile strategy for any brand. Please answer each question by assigning it a score ranging from 1 to 3.

1 = Not Important
2 = Somewhat Important
3 = Very Important

#### Mobile Apps

| Question | Score |
|---|---|
| 1. How important is having mobile strategy for your brand? | |
| 2. Do you see your business releasing or updating an existing mobile app in the next 1–2 years? | |
| 3. Is driving app conversion an essential part of your marketing efforts? | |
| 4. How critical is it for your business to offer a seamless experience on iOS, Android, and the mobile web? | |
| 5. Do you plan to create loyalty or rewards programs using a mobile app? | |

#### In-Store Technology

| Question | Score |
|---|---|
| 1. How important is it for your business to have mobile technology in store? | |
| 2. Do you consider mobile-enabled associates a must for your brand? | |
| 3. Is digital clienteling an essential part of your store strategy? | |

| | |
|---|---|
| 4. How important is mobile point-of-sale for your store success? | |
| 5. How critical are digitally savvy associates for your stores? | |

**Fulfillment**

| Question | Score |
|---|---|
| 1. Are modern fulfillment options such as on-demand delivery important to your customers? | |
| 2. Do you have, or envision, stores playing a critical role as fulfillment centers for your business? | |
| 3. Is offering Buy Online Pick Up in Store (BOPIS) and Buy Online Return in Store (BORIS) an essential part of servicing your customers? | |
| 4. Is fulfillment considered an essential part of your customer loyalty and retention strategy? | |
| 5. Is fulfillment used as a competitive advantage for your brand? | |

**Analytics**

| Question | Score |
|---|---|
| 1. How important are omnichannel data collection and analysis for your brand? | |
| 2. Is data-driven analysis of key performance indicators for each department an essential part of your day-to-day operation? | |
| 3. Does your brand use or plan to use data-driven insights for mobile success? | |

### Retail Organization

| Question | Score |
|---|---|
| 1. How essential is it for your brand to tie store associates' compensation to omnichannel success instead of to store sales? | |
| 2. How essential is it for your brand to tie store managers' compensation to omnichannel success instead of to store sales? | |
| 3. Are your stores sharing, or will they share, stock with online stores or the online marketplace? | |

### IT System Landscape

| Question | Score |
|---|---|
| 1. Is having an inventory management system that can provide live stock information from all stores and distribution centers a must-have for your daily operations? | |
| 2. Is managing product master data, price tables, and product-related media assets in one system part of your business practice today? | |
| 3. Is a robust order management system that handles orders from multiple channels part of your business today? | |

What do your results tell you?

Calculate your total score.

57–72 Points: Ready for Mobile
You are aware of all facets of your business that require transformation, and perhaps some of them have already been transformed. Your business is able to move forward with building and executing your mobile strategy with all the important pieces of the puzzle that make up the mobile landscape in place.

41–56 Points: Getting Started with Mobile
Your organization is not fully ripe for mobile transformation. Examine your answers and ask why you gave individual areas a score of lower importance. Have these areas been reduced in importance over other priorities? If so, are these other priorities essential for customer relationship success?

24–40 Points: Considering Mobile
Your brand might not be in a position to embrace mobile transformation just yet. Making the mobile shift takes a tremendous amount of time and resources. This assessment will help you navigate the areas that need to be addressed for mobile success.

## *Conclusion: The Opportunity of the S Curve*

This chapter began with a discussion of the Hype Cycle. It ends with another graph to consider, the Innovation S Curve.

Transformation, we know, does not travel in a clean straight line. There are often muddled periods when it isn't clear which way is up. In our research for our *Mobile Retail Report*, we found that only 22% of the retailers we surveyed offer mobile apps that can be used for making purchases. An additional 22% have non-shoppable apps that show products or have other features but do not allow transactions to be completed through the app. What's more, we found that few retailers take full advantage of mobile technology such as push notifications (64%), Touch ID (29%), and universal linking (8%). Nonetheless, this is starting to change as more retailers experiment with new technology. As mobile works its way through the retail industry, the reality of the Innovation S Curve becomes obvious. The curve shows a new technology emerging, converging, and then overtaking an old technology. That's where we are now in the mobile versus desktop web shopping story. There is a period at which old and new technologies will overlap and co-mingle. Looking around at the retail landscape, you could argue that's where we find ourselves now, at a place where web shopping and mobile shopping are both part of the shopping experience. The question is, which way is up?

To answer that, look at the shoppers in your stores today. When they walk in, what are they holding? When they wait for help at the register, what are they holding? When they walk down the street in front of your store, what are they holding?

## The S Curve in Commerce: Brands Leading the Next Turn in the S Curve Will Thrive

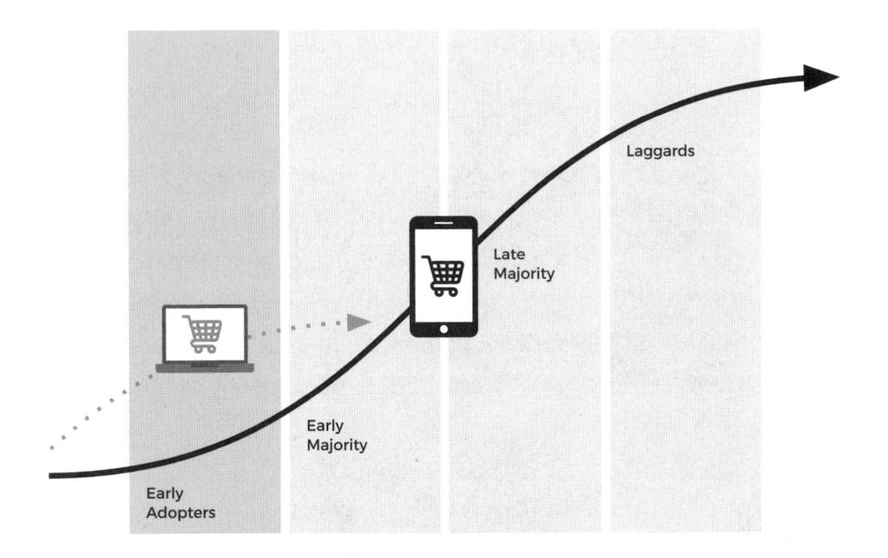


Mobile is here. Mobile is already part of the shopping experience because it's already part of the shopper's experience. The question to be addressed by CTOs thus becomes, "Can we make this experience better for shoppers?"

Some stores are already testing this. Some already have their CTOs oriented toward the three-pronged process of innovation, experimentation, and strategy. They will be the retailers leading the next turn in the Innovation S Curve.

# Mobile Transformation in the Making

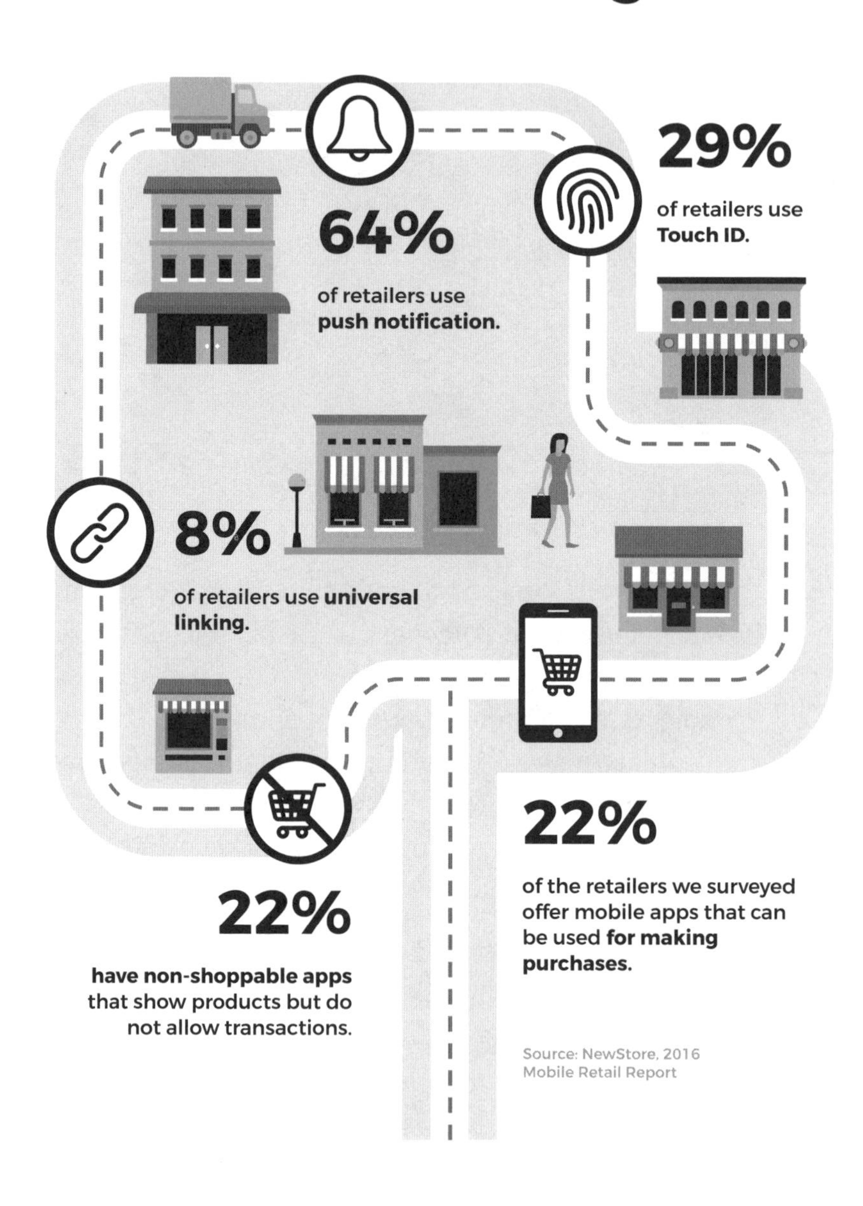

## *To Wrap Up:*

- Conduct a comprehensive analysis to identify the areas you want to address with a technology makeover. Research and planning will take longer than any other aspect.
- Embrace the partnership approach to a mobile technology makeover for your brand. If you decide to do it solo, research all the costs associated with attracting and keeping the talent in house.
- Experimentation is key to understanding what technology will work best for your brand and for your customers.

## *Next Steps:*

- Look at your strategy. How can mobile technology be part of executing your larger plans?
- Consider your brand promise. How will your decisions around mobile technology affect your brand promise? What do your customers expect from you when it comes to new technology, and how does your mobile strategy fit with that vision?
- Watch your competition. What are your competitors doing in the mobile space, and what are their results? Consider both your close competition and also companies and even industries that might seem far afield. Best practices might emerge in another industry that are applicable to your experience.

- Gather research advice. Experts in the field are distributing data and recommendations. Be sure you are up to date on the latest thought leadership and research data as you plot your own mobile path forward.
- Be prepared to experiment. The world of mobile is evolving. New technologies and functionalities are on the rise. Customers are also evolving in their tastes regarding mobile, testing and experimenting with the new elements and deciding what they like and dislike. Be prepared to experiment and learn with your customer. Mobile transformation is a work in progress.

## Voices from the Mobile Makeover

*Robert Gentz, Co-CEO, Zalando*

Zalando, an online fashion retailer, has a unique perspective on the influence of mobile on the fashion business. Of course, Robert Gentz's business is already mobile, with 50% of his visits coming from mobile devices. But his perspective on mobile is not only a view of his own business.

Often, it's not what technology a fashion brand uses that makes the difference. It's how well the brand understands how technology impacts the shopping world.

"I think if you haven't pivoted to mobile, you haven't observed where customer behavior is," Gentz notes. Yet, as brands enter the mobile space, they might find the landscape isn't what they expected.

For example, Gentz says, a strong consumer brand doesn't necessarily help a company generate a high mobile reach. If you look at the most downloaded apps, you'll see they aren't the big consumer brands. They are the apps made for mobile. Consequently, he explains, the consumer brand won't help in mobile as much as it might have in the web world. To manage that reality, brands need to think about what is effective on the small screen. How do you involve influencers? How do you use video? Gentz concludes, "These are elements that are native to mobile, and they are the ones you will need to tell your brand story."

Chapter 7

# The Data Relationship Makeover

**Insights**

- Mobile allows retailers to collect and use data in stores, with shoppers, in real time.
- Privacy issues will be addressed as customers experience data collection and decide for all of us where the limits lie.
- Making data-driven decisions should be part of every retailer's day-to-day operations.

*Go into a store and consider this: you can't hear it, but the computers are talking.*

In today's connected age, computers are rarely out of contact with their networks. It is unusual to come across a "dumb" terminal – one with no contact with the outside information world. Screens are connected and always on.

This truism extends to the screens in our pockets. The advent of smartphones means that, every day, we carry pocket-sized computers with us. Like most computers we come across, our palm-sized computers communicate. No matter what we're doing with them at any given moment, chances are good our smartphones are reaching out into the technological ecosystem. Maybe they're looking for a Wi-Fi network to join. Perhaps they're installing updates or refreshing content. They're always on, always looking to converse with other computers.

That hardly stops when you enter a store. In fact, when you walk into a store today, big computers are talking to small computers and the exchange of data is happening even as you check out the displays and browse through the racks. The computers are talking about you, and your store experience is the better for it.

This is an important way mobile is transforming the data relationship in the retail world. It isn't happening in some server farm or in a research department at company headquarters. Mobile is transforming data by making the data collectable and usable in the store environment.

## *Mobile Has Flipped Data*

Data has long been vital to the retail industry, but it has often been cast as a player best suited to strategic planning. Data is the tool kit retailers turn to in order to predict and understand trends, make smart capital investments, and make sense of the industry at large. Data, especially as it came to be called Big Data, was very much a big-picture process.

Use of data became more granular in the internet age as connected computers gave retailers the opportunity to track individuals and technology created ways to craft targeted offers. While consumers bristled a bit at the thought of being virtually followed online, they also responded positively to receiving relevant ads.

Now, mobile has come to data and transformed the amount of information that can be collected and the way it can be used by retailers. This is both the promise and the challenge – retailers are wrestling with both sides of the mobile data transformation. The key is to understand what they need in order to make data-driven decisions.

## *Mobile Can Follow Feet*

Retailers can use mobile-enabled foot traffic technology to find out where consumers go when they enter a store. Certainly, store associates can see where shoppers go as they browse, but mobile technology can offer data and analysis, not just anecdotal evidence, that results in more than just store associate observations but in actual actionable insights.

Some mobile-enabled foot trackers offer A/B testing to review variations. The Cellular Connection conducted a series of A/B tests to refine the sale of high-margin accessories such as chargers and headsets. The tests revealed these items sold in much greater numbers when moved from the back of the store to the front and a change in layout was implemented. Another retailer in New York City used A/B testing to determine which offerings – discount coupons, free coffee, etc. – would encourage shoppers to climb to its upper floors instead of simply remaining on the main level[18].

How else can mobile transform the use of data?

# Beacon-Generated Data Can...

**Extend loyalty programs**

**Combine real-time and historical data**

**Empower sales associates**

**Offer dynamic sales and couponing**

## *Mobile Enhances In-Store Personalization*

Beacons are one of the least understood new technologies that will help usher companies into the next generation of retail.

In general, four conditions must be met in order for beacons to work. First, the beacon needs to be transmitting. Second, the customer's mobile device needs to be on with Bluetooth enabled. Third, the customer needs to have the retailer's mobile app installed. Finally, the customer needs to have already given permission for the app to share location data (this usually occurs at installation).

What most consumers and retailers alike don't know is that the app doesn't have to be running in order for the device to be recognized, its location tracked, and messages delivered. Once beacons are in place, they can be leveraged in virtually endless ways to serve up a better in-store experience by delivering a stream of data that can be used on the spot by a retail associate or later by trend seekers crunching numbers and looking for trends.

### What can beacon-generated data do?

1. Extend loyalty programs. The same location-based technology could be used to seamlessly reward a customer for visiting a real-life storefront or even for browsing a certain product. Imagine the following enticement: "Drop by any of our stores and earn five bonus dollars that can be redeemed toward future purchases."

2. Empower sales associates. The communication that beacons facilitate doesn't have to be device to device.

Once a beacon notices a known customer, that information can be shared with sales associates so they can greet that customer by name, if that's the customer's preference.

3. Combine real-time and historical data. In the example above, not only could customers be recognized and greeted by name, but also the sales associates could be made aware of the customers' last few purchases as well as the items they recently placed in their online/mobile shopping carts, or any items they virtually browsed.
4. Offer dynamic sales and couponing. Because the beacon can track a device's location within a couple of feet, customers can be offered a discount or alerted to a sale right as they pass an item.

Beacons are an area of opportunity for retailers, as we discovered in our *Mobile Retail Report*. When it came to personalization and creating an engaging experience, almost all retailers offered options to create accounts, with 94% of retailers offering it on their mobile websites, 5% offering separate loyalty accounts, and 88% offering the account creation on their iOS apps and 100% on their Android apps. However, none of the retailers we audited enlisted beacon technology to help associates determine who their customers were and when their customers entered the brick-and-mortar store.

Even if the store is using cutting-edge technology, the transformation of data in the retail environment comes with challenges.

## *Solving Problems with Data*

Perhaps most significant, there is so much data – and now so many ways to capture it – that retailers are scrambling to figure out what they want from all this information.

Every business owner likes to think about maximized foot traffic and consistent profits. Technology certainly holds a key to achieving these, but using technology for its own sake can be a fruitless exercise.

Some devices, even those that look most exciting, are still just "solutions in search of a problem." For each, the question remains, "What does the retailer want to get out of it?" There must be a direct connection between the systems and the customer, and that connection is data. After all, data best measures success.

All commerce-related information, whether amassed through an online site, in the store, or both, should be tied to the problems the retailer is trying to solve. It must match in some way to the goal of understanding the customer and supporting the brand. It must cure pain and deliver benefits. This starts with baseline data, to which analysis is afterward applied. Retailers must figure out what it is they want to do and then leverage the technology to do it. This helps ensure that the results can be translated and applied.

There has never been a better time to use technology to measure success in the world of retail. At the same time, retailers face the challenge of deciding what to measure and then with data in hand, what to do next. In the early days of ecommerce, when retailers talked about data, they meant sitting at a desktop while gathering and examining the information generated by customers. Today, mobile has transformed the data possibilities. Now we travel with our computers in our hands. We are rarely without them. For that reason, the possibilities of data have fundamentally changed.

Timelines and costs have shrunk considerably. In the pre-mobile days, technological innovation required massive upfront investments paired with equally costly implementation, but new models, hosted in the cloud, are changing this. The chief investment now is in people rather than machinery. When a highly evolved and carefully chosen software solution is paired with mobile-enabled staff, it changes the route and the time to profitability for the better.

Another critical element in measuring success is that much of the data will come primarily from technologies consumers are already familiar with. Regarding immediate ROI, retailers should look at the supercomputing power customers already hold in their hands – their smartphones – and strive to leverage it in a way that gives these customers new types of interactions. These could be exchanges customers haven't yet experienced in a sales transaction with one retailer but might have experienced with another.

Snapchat is a good example. What would it be like if Snapchat became the facilitator between a sales associate and a consumer for a quick sale? New types of connections can be made through the tools already sitting in people's hands. Success then might not necessarily be about digitizing the store so much as it is about taking advantage of the digital relationship that already exists between the consumer, the store, and the store associate. Rent the Runway, for example, uses Snapchat to help customers find the right fit. When Rent the Runway receives a snap, one of its employees who best fits the customer's size and height tries on the dress and posts a video wearing it.

Successful use of data demands appropriate observations. Retailers must decide on their focus area, such as simplifying the shopping experience or engaging customers. They must observe their customers and look for patterns and then use that data to drive decisions. What they must try to avoid, however, is the potential for "data smog."

Everything is measurable, from where people stand in the store to how frequently they abandon potential clothing purchases in the dressing rooms. This means there will be a lot of data to look at, and too much data creates a fog that wastes time and resources. Thus, the role of data scientists in retail will become much more important since these are the people best qualified to sort out and interpret the numbers.

This is retail coming full circle. Success has always been based on how well products sell and the profitability of the store. Although the bottom line is still important – it's a business after all – many non-financial tools such as data drive revenues. This is perhaps a less linear path, but profit remains the goal.

## *Key Challenge: Making Data Work*

Retailers face another set of problems when it comes to data: how to manage the complex world of data analytics. Far too often, the analytics process devolves into glorified reporting. Data is collected, sorted, and distributed, but it fails to deliver on the most important benefit: delivering insights.

The true goal of data collection is ultimately better decision making. When you can get past reporting the data and engage in the process of gleaning insights, data boosts your business. Still, this is often the point at which retailers stumble. The data is gathered but the insights lag.

Forrester Research finds that the path forward is complicated. One of the biggest challenges, the research firm found, is that projects in retail analytics are often launched without clearly defined use cases[19].

The instinct to collect data is present, and the fact that customers are coming in carrying Wi-Fi and Bluetooth makes it possible, but a clear use case is often absent. Even when retailers make a strong case, complications arise when the new data must be married to other enterprise data. With two sets of data, how do you meld these two sources into a coherent strategy? Forrester suggests defining the value customers will receive via tracked behavior, testing data collection in a single store before rolling it out, defining goals before launching a project, and planning ahead for how stores will access and leverage the collected information.

## *Wearables Offer a Window to the Future*

How will this tension between privacy and data collection play out in the mobile retail space? For clues, watch the experience of wearables.

From watches to jewelry to sneakers with sensors, wearables are a good example of how mobile can offer new options for data collection to retailers as well as new benefits to customers. Wearables are fashion items embedded with technology that collects and transmits data. These mobile devices are always on, always talking to other computers, always collecting and sending data about the user to the brand. Fitbit is perhaps the most famous of the group, but many brands have followed its lead.

Swarovski, for example, sells a wearable device with its signature crystals adorning the mobile data collector. Placed in a pendant ring or worn on the wrist, this device is designed, the company says, to work for the woman who dresses up for meetings in the morning but might go work out in the afternoon. The data collection is designed not on steps but on a "points" system; i.e., 1,000 points could be reached by 1.5 hours of walking or 30 minutes of running.

Michael Kors has launched a line of wearables in the form of smart watches that have a host of functions: touchscreen display for social media, text and email alerts, app notifications, fitness tracking, and, from Google's "smart help" and voice activation.

Tory Burch sells a line of Fitbit-compatible bracelets and pendants, all upscale versions of the rubber Fitbit options most of the trackers come packaged in. Perfect for exercise, but not for your modern day consumer who wants to put fashion first.

So far, wearables focus on the fitness concept, but there's no reason a wearable can't branch out into other activities.

That computer in your pocket is always talking. Mobile is making data gathering easier, faster, and far more vast in scope. Brands will need to work with customers to find out the balance needed to make the technology a positive experience.

## *Privacy Concerns Loom Large*

Even while customers interact daily with brands, privacy concerns remain. Research firm L2 notes that brands walk a fine line as they seek to collect data while at the same time building trust with their customers. It doesn't help that customers are giving off decidedly mixed signals in this area. On the one hand, L2 research shows that shoppers want to receive relevant messages from retailers. On the other hand, shoppers believe their data is being sold and shared and that they, the customers, are not receiving benefits through personalized service. The picture isn't at all clear, which gives brands pause as they wade into mobile data opportunities[20].

But privacy concerns should not scare retailers away from exploring mobile transformation for data. This exploration is necessary to lead to new standards. When it comes to mobile technology, just how "personal" must things get before enough is enough? When will people collectively draw a line in the sand and say, "I want no further connection between technology and me"?

My feeling is that the line will continue to move just slightly in front of us. Collectively, I do not believe we want to put the brakes on our digital involvement.

At this moment in time, we are watching the computer users of the world – who recently said goodbye to their bulky desktop computers – pull the plug on their laptops in order to embrace the next generation of mobile devices that attach to or travel with the body with very little effort. These devices have become the essential new connection point between our individual selves and the collective digital tribe to which we all want to belong.

In the face of this collective fascination, there is paradoxically a sense of fear among many that innovations in technology have perhaps become too intrusive. Beacon sensors are an example of this. Beacons are designed to notice when specific customers enter a store, and they allow the store's customer management system to retrieve that customer's shopping preferences. Some people, upon hearing this for the first time, find it intrusive or downright creepy, especially when the beacons are placed inside store mannequins. There is something dystopian about this, at least at first blush.

As with so much of the mobile economy, these developments deliver unprecedented levels of convenience. Any shopper who has rebuffed a sales associate's offer to help with the phrase, "No thanks, just browsing," or has wandered the aisles of a big-box store looking for some guidance will quickly appreciate the accessibility of an unobtrusive yet directly useful assistant.

The sharing of the data that makes beacon technology work is purely voluntary. Just like the privacy settings on your phone and social media accounts, digital loyalty programs are there for customers to use as they choose. Customers who don't want to play shouldn't.

Consumer interest is a key concept to consider when looking at the larger notion of the "Uber-ization of Retail," the subject of an article I wrote for *Internet Retailer*[21]. Uber is a crowdsourced approach to personal transportation that takes on the traditional taxicab industry by eliminating the middleman and communicating directly with the consumer – if, and only if, the consumer chooses to use Uber. There are plenty of other choices of transport always available.

Obviously, the implications of Uber-ization go well beyond taxi services. They usher in a newly personal shopping experience in which customers leverage the power of their own data to enjoy more tailored and satisfactory events.

The fear of intrusive data is a perfectly normal human response often followed by acceptance that evolves into enthusiasm. The smartphone is a perfect example of this. For most consumers, its versatility and convenience vastly eclipse any personal privacy issues initially felt about the phone's presence on a cellular network. Consumers have, in large measure, willingly bypassed the idea that their every move is trackable and photographable in exchange for the irresistible comfort and versatility of their smart devices.

The Uber-ization of retail is about the further democratization of consumerism in which individuals enjoy greater personal leverage and receive a heightened degree of tailored service, all on their own terms.

Protecting personal data is a skill that consumers can choose to learn and perfect, a form of digital literacy in which privacy and choice are the key building blocks of their own experience. These skills need to be learned and practiced, just like using an ATM or giving out credit card numbers over the phone. These are skills and choices that individuals own. We allow the data to be released in order to reap rewards and convenience. That's the currency of modern commerce – the Uber-ization of a centuries-old practice.

## *To Wrap Up:*

- Mobile technology vastly expands the amount of data that can be collected. While this is good news, it also raises the potential specter of data overload. Retailers will need to decide what they want to know and why. Collecting data without strategic goals yields glorified reporting rather than true analytics used to make data-driven decisions.

- Mobile allows data to be collected and used in stores. Store associates can be armed to gather and make use of data on the spot. Beacon technology allows retailers to capture shoppers' movements in real time. Mobile CRM allows store associates to see shoppers' histories and make personalized recommendations on the store floor.

- Privacy remains a concern, but understanding customers' tolerance levels requires experimentation and research. We will not know how far customers will go until we give them new experiences and let them tell us what they think and want. As with many technological innovations, it will be our real-life experiences with new technology that ultimately reveal our limits. While shoppers might seem hesitant at first about privacy issues, often a positive experience with sharing data changes minds and tolerances.

## *Next Steps:*

- Define goals before collecting new data. This is the best way to help graduate from standard data reporting to the richer experience of data analytics. Without goals, collected and warehoused data might not serve your company goals.
- Set success measurements for data collection. How will you know if your data efforts are successful? Like anything else in a good company, data measurement needs KPIs.
- Understand the benefit to customers of new data collection efforts. What can more data do for your customers? Be sure you consider that concept yourself as well as communicate it to customers. Shoppers will be more willing to share data when they see the direct benefit to their experiences. On the flip side, if shoppers cannot see any benefit, they will be less likely to agree to participate and share data.
- Test new data collection in a single store before rolling out the project. Take time to determine what data can be harvested, how that data can be used to gain insights, and how your customers react to the process on a small scale before taking it to the full company.

## Voices from the Mobile Makeover

*Harm Ohlmeyer, Chief Financial Officer (former SVP Digital Brand), adidas*

As much as mobile data collection can tell us, some find the traditional focus group useful when trying to understand transformation in the mobile age.

Harm Ohlmeyer of adidas Group says that often the information from focus groups is striking in its clear message to retailers. He said, "We had a focus group of people in LA ages 17 to 25. One young woman told us exactly how mobile technology will change the retail landscape. She said she doesn't bother to go to a store in a mall because she knows that 98% of what is in that store is irrelevant to her and it's hard work to find that 2%. Instead, she goes to her smartphone. The app filters the content for her, and she only has to see the 2% that is relevant to her. Of course, this makes perfect sense, but it's a huge challenge to the physical store."

Top challenges Ohlmeyer sees as he works to transform his company for the mobile age include attracting talent: "In the past, we were in competition with Nike and Puma for the best talent. Now we also must compete with the tech companies, Google, Apple, and Facebook, to attract the talent we need."

Getting staff to go mobile first: "We are looking at a next generation of customers, and they grew up with iPhones. They are mobile first, so we must be mobile first, not just in our customer experience but in our company. We all need to train ourselves to be mobile first. When we create a piece of content on a desktop, it's a desktop experience. It's not easy to change and create on the mobile screen, but this is the learning we're getting from customers who are using the smartphone. Mobile first starts with us."

*Chapter 8*

# The Fulfillment Relationship Makeover

**Insights**

- Fulfillment is an opportunity to surprise and delight customers.
- New industries such as ridesharing have flipped expectations and now offer new fulfillment options.

Amazon is the biggest question mark in retail. Its influence is only growing. From its humble roots as an online bookstore, the company now launches its own brands and is even expected to emerge as the largest clothing retailer in the U.S. Some brands are scared. Some are confident. Some are ignoring Amazon's moves. We believe it's important to pay attention to the company's business but more importantly to the expectations it sets with consumers.

Today, consumers expect quick and seamless delivery, payment, and customer service on almost any purchase. Brands big and small are now competing with these expectations.

That said, brands are not fighting to beat Amazon. That would be futile. Instead, brands need to rise to the level of convenience that Amazon has led millions of customers to expect. To do this, retailers need to differentiate their experience and leverage their physical footprints to speed up delivery and unlock as much inventory as possible. In other words, they need to focus on flipping fulfillment.

Amazon has vulnerabilities when it comes to moving merchandise. Jet.com perceived that many of Amazon's products are shipped in a less than economical manner. Jet.com developed a dynamic formula that takes into account factors such as basket size, shipping options, and merchandise proximity to buyers. Using that, Jet.com was able to undercut Amazon in price. This clever move helped convince Walmart to pay $3 billion to acquire Jet.com.

There is room for other retailers to challenge Amazon. As mobile has flipped the shopping cart and disrupted retail, it has opened new opportunities to challenge Amazon's monopoly on convenience. Many of these opportunities occur after the sale. This requires rethinking the fulfillment concept, and it starts by looking at fulfillment not just as a physical process but also as part of the customer experience, one that can be enhanced and leveraged. When retailers begin to see fulfillment as an occasion for an emotional bond rather than just a logistics process, the opportunities appear.

The chief enabler of satisfactory fulfillment is the native mobile app. There is tremendous potential for bringing shoppers, stores, and delivery mechanisms together on the same point on the planet, at the right time. Some enterprising retailers are already experimenting with crowdsourced services such as UberRUSH and Deliv, though for most this opportunity is untapped. Our research for our *Mobile Retail Report* showed that last-mile delivery of digital purchases is rare, with only 2% of retailers offering that option to urban and suburban locations within a few hours of purchase. Growing pains still need to be worked through, but the notion of a parcel converging with a customer on a street corner, in a coffee shop, or wherever the customer happens to be at any given moment is not so outrageous.

Shoppers' own mobile technology including geolocation, QR codes, and an app connected to the dispatching store has the capacity to smooth out the intricacies of the handoff. The payments, confirmations, and any other retail fulfillment details travel through the ether. All the driver has to do is locate, identify, and confirm the recipient, deliver the goods, and move on.

With details yet to be worked out, this highly mobile, personal, and agile fulfillment of the purchase process holds great potential for any retailer who wishes to beat Amazon at its own game by delivering an even better and more personal level of convenience simply as a dividend of being small.

## Stop Saying "The Last Mile"

Retail likes to use the phrase "the last mile" in its discussion of delivery. I used it several times myself on the previous page. This catchphrase describing the stage of the customer journey at which the product or service lands in the customer's hands has been around for decades.

It has to go. The very language holds the industry back. The problem is the word "last." What if we thought of the interaction between the retailer and customer as a never-ending circle? Imagine a relationship in which the retailer or brand is in constant service to a customer, and a customer is in constant connection with his or her favorite brand. What if there were no "last"? What might that look like?

## The Hub and Spoke Method

Mobile commerce can resolve "the last mile" problem by handing it over to customers in ways that will not only leave them satisfied but also give them the opportunity to shop more. The process allows consumers to shop virtually via desktop or mobile and then pick up the item at a store.

Some retailers are experimenting with the "hub and spoke" model in which the larger of their stores pulls double duty as brick-and-mortar locations and hub warehouses. These then feed a half-dozen "spoke" stores where people can go pick up their products.

The hub and spoke model also helps deal with another nagging problem in the brick-and-mortar retail industry: locations that are doomed to close due to slow business. These locations have the opportunity to be born anew as satellite spots for fulfillment in a new mobile commerce-led economy.

This model has the potential to become widespread. Many malls house empty stores that would be perfectly suited for this type of customer pickup system. Just like anchor tenants, there would be great potential for other stores to leverage the revitalized customer traffic.

Some U.K. retailers are already experimenting with this method. A recent Insight Report by L2 entitled "Retail Innovations: Omnichannel" shows that nearly twice as many European department stores offer this pickup feature as do stores in the U.S.[22]. The major chain John Lewis states that it fulfills 54% of its online orders this way, something it has been doing since 2008.

Hub and spoke fulfillment might even help suburban shopping malls. Many malls that rose up in the pre-internet era have struggled to stay relevant while being buffeted by many trends. Some are weakened by anchor tenants that no longer maintain their dominance and draw in the modern retail age. Others suffer from the competition offered by virtual shopping – why drive to the mall when you can click online?

But hub and spoke offers a solution to this problem. Consider this scenario:

Amanda is up early, making breakfast, and opens up her smartphone to surf for back-to-school clothing for her three girls. It's a sunny summer morning, and her kids are playing in the yard as she shops. One by one, she brings each girl in to look over the merchandise options and make choices. When the youngest won't come in off the swings, Amanda takes the phone outside and lets her daughter shop from the swing set.

Amanda could opt for overnight shipping, but during this online session, she receives a personalized offer from the restaurant at her nearby regional shopping center. She opts for in-store pickup, and when lunchtime nears, she piles her girls into the car and heads for the mall.

After parking, she heads for the restaurant. As they are seated and looking at menus, Amanda takes out her smartphone and selects the mall's free valet pick-and-pack service. The family enjoys lunch and discusses the back-to-school events that will be taking place in the coming weeks. As the girls chatter, Amanda marvels at how big they've become and snaps a picture on her smartphone to send to her mother.

Meanwhile, throughout the mall, the back-to-school items are being readied. All the stores received Amanda's order hours earlier, so associates were able to check and see if they had the items in stock. When the shoe retailer associate realized there were no sparkly shoes on her shelves, she was able to use her company's mobile inventory visibility to locate them at another store and arrange delivery to the mall location. Similarly, the children's clothing store did not have some items in the less popular sizes but was able to connect with its downtown location and have the items sent to the mall.

With lunch eaten, Amanda and her girls head for the mall's pickup location. All their packages are neatly packed and waiting. As Amanda is preparing to leave, she receives another alert on her smartphone, this one from her favorite store at the mall. They are having a sale, so Amanda asks the pickup location to hold her bags a little while longer. She makes a visit to her favorite retailer, where she makes several purchases.

After she collects her packages, she heads for the parking garage. Everyone piles in, and the youngest asks if she can change into her sparkly shoes in the car. Amanda pulls out of the parking lot pleased to have the back-to-school shopping mission accomplished!

Deploying mobile enhances the customer experience. Certainly, Amanda could have opted for overnight delivery, which would have saved her the trouble of shopping, but mobile stepped in and allowed that experience to transform from "acceptable" to "memorable."

## *On-Demand Delivery*

When you come to the end of an Amazon shopping experience, you'll be offered some options: shipping methods of varying lengths and price and, if you're a Prime customer in a certain area, same day delivery.

Thanks to ecommerce, customers have learned to expect delivery options. Research has found that 26% of shoppers are willing to pay $10 or more for same day delivery, 13% would pay extra for next-day delivery, and 22% would consider paying $20 or more for delivery within two hours[23].

Other consumers want their purchases fast and free, with easier return and replacement when needed. While Amazon Prime maintains a stronghold over one-hour delivery choices (the Amazon Prime Now app lets customers browse products that are available for rush delivery), brands should still aim to provide mobile users with a slew of shipping preferences to enable them to receive their packages overnight, if they choose, or in a more standard time frame. Teaming up with a third-party delivery app could be a beneficial strategy to look into, particularly if a marketer is having difficulty guaranteeing speedy shipping.

Amazon is the king of leveraging shipping as a competitive advantage. When it launched its Amazon Prime service in 2005, it took the ecommerce world by storm by lessening some of the larger hindrances to buying products online – the cost of shipping and the inconvenience of frequently having to wait five or more days to receive an order. In the decade since its inception, Amazon Prime has increased the loyalty and average spending of those Amazon customers who subscribe to it. One study conducted by

Consumer Intelligence Research Partners in 2013 shows that the average Prime customer spends $1,340 dollars per year on the retailer's website, more than double the $650 the average non-Prime customer spends[24].

Traditional retailers are jumping in by partnering with delivery services. Deliv, for example, powers same day delivery from a range of national retail partners including Macys, Bloomingdales, Best Buy, Kohls, Google Express, and BloomThat. Shoppers simply select same day delivery at checkout. Deliv is connected to retailers' ecommerce systems via their application program interface, or API, and orders are seamlessly passed along. The retailer picks and packs the items, and the Deliv driver picks up the orders from the designated store and delivers them during the chosen time frame. This turns all those stores or businesses into fulfillment centers.

In addition to getting orders directly through their API, retailers can also schedule deliveries via a service such as UberRUSH or Deliv from their stores via an online portal. Retailers can also offer delivery windows to their customers, who can then select the window that works best for them. Some delivery services will also act as a couriers for returns.

This should not come as a surprise, as product delivery is an integral part of the overall customer experience. It determines how quickly customers start using and enjoying a product and also how quickly they can begin acting as brand ambassadors for the company that sells the product. Mobile can transform fulfillment by multiplying the delivery options, allowing retailers the flexibility to craft personally designed fulfillment plans for every individual shopper.

There are options when using mobile for fulfillment. You can tell the brand what you want, and a mobile-engaged retailer makes it happen. Hugo Boss, for example, has partnered with Shoprunner to offer free two-day shipping. Hugo Boss also allows consumers to designate, at online checkout, a retail outlet for pickup and alterations.

In many ways, this is all about options. Innovative brands such as Outdoor Voices set up their stores as fulfillment centers in the basement, with the retail store on the first floor and corporate offices on the second floor. This gives shoppers choices. They can have all items shipped to their home address, or, if they prefer, the items can be delivered to another location at a later time that day via an on-demand delivery service. By using mobile to expand fulfillment options, technology offers customers the flexibility they want.

## *Curbside*

Curbside offers another opportunity for mobile transformation. Curbside customer pickup provides a tangible touch point with customers while reducing delivery times and eliminating shipping costs. A poll by *Internet Retailer* found avoiding shipping costs to be the most popular reason for in-store pickup, followed by the convenience of a nearby store and the desire to have the item right away[25]. Stores also have the opportunity to benefit from this trend.

The Insight Report by L2 shows that this touch point can register a 7% gain in net sales due to additional opportunities for the store to interact with customers[26]. Customers might receive personalized discounts on their mobile devices as they enter the parking lot. Perhaps the associate who handles the physical delivery of the item is empowered to make the additional offer. Or perhaps great signage encourages customers to park and come in to look around, participate in an in-store event, or make another purchase.

If we look at this moment of delivery not as a "last" element of the customer journey but as a point on a circle, the experience takes on new meaning and new opportunity. Through mobile, brands can continue to communicate.

## *Buy Online, Pick up in Store*

In the U.S., some coffee shops already offer customers the option of placing their orders from their phones before entering the store to pick them up. The same concept now applies to retail stores through curbside pickup programs. This is an interesting take on "the last mile" concept, that crucial distance that completes the transaction between vendor and customer.

Current statistics show digital consumers return 20%–30% of their apparel purchases[27].

When retailers offer the "buy online/pick up in store" option, the return rate drops. When this is further refined to "buy online/return in store," the revenue potential jumps because of the additional impulse or routine purchases.

Still, integrating mobile into the buy online/pick up in store option remains a work in progress. Our research for our *Mobile Retail Report* found that while 13% of the brands we researched offered the buy online/pick up in store option, none of them allowed transactions started in the app or on the mobile website to be completed in store.

## ***The Opportunity: Meeting (and Beating) Amazon Expectations***

Amazon is an entity that conveniently dispenses and delivers products without human intervention. It has strengths, but it also has limitations. As vast and efficient as Amazon is, it can be a brand-dissolving mechanism.

First, there's the customer's perspective. Amazon does not provide sales associates who understand and love the brand and its products. Amazon merely responds to requests. Certain consumables sell well through this model, specifically items with a previously established value statement such as books and videos, tunes by a favorite artist, or even bags of grass seed. However, many purchases depend on the interaction between consumers and knowledgeable sales associates to balance choices and preferences and get the right "fit." The more personal the item – such as a computer mouse or a pair of shoes – the wider the gap and the narrower the opportunity for an emotionally satisfying transaction.

Second, there's the retailer's perspective. Merchandise might see its hard-won brand fade substantially under the overpowering presence of Amazon's influence. Items are arranged courtesy of price and search history algorithms. Competing products of varying quality appear *en masse*, rendering them anonymous in the process.

It's a mistake to think technology reduces the high-touch experience. In truth, technology can increase it, placing other sellers at the polar opposite of Amazon's approach. Retail, after all, is theater. It's a physical and emotional event organized for the satisfaction of each customer. The best real-world stores such as Nike, Apple, adidas, or Jimmy Choo already deliver a finely executed service that contributes to the overall enjoyment of the purchase. Now, other retailers are deploying tools that augment human contact and assist brands in providing some of their value through the experience of acquiring the product.

For example, a major shoe brand uses the on-demand delivery service to fulfill orders for a new product within four hours of the order placement. The orders are placed by consumers using a mobile app and received via the fulfillment app by the stockroom workers who pick, pack, and arrange for a car driver to deliver the orders to the customers' specified locations. Customers are notified about each step of the journey and can see the estimated delivery time and even the car driver delivering their shoes on the map within their branded app.

This is a one-of-a-kind experience that can be enabled by mobile, but our research shows that not everyone is taking advantage of this possibility. As our *Mobile Retail Report* revealed, just 22% of retailers in our study offered in-store pickup options on the shopping app, and only 4% offered rapid delivery via the app using a ridesharing or delivery service.

Fulfillment, assisted by mobile technology, isn't just the last mile. It's another opportunity to delight the customer.

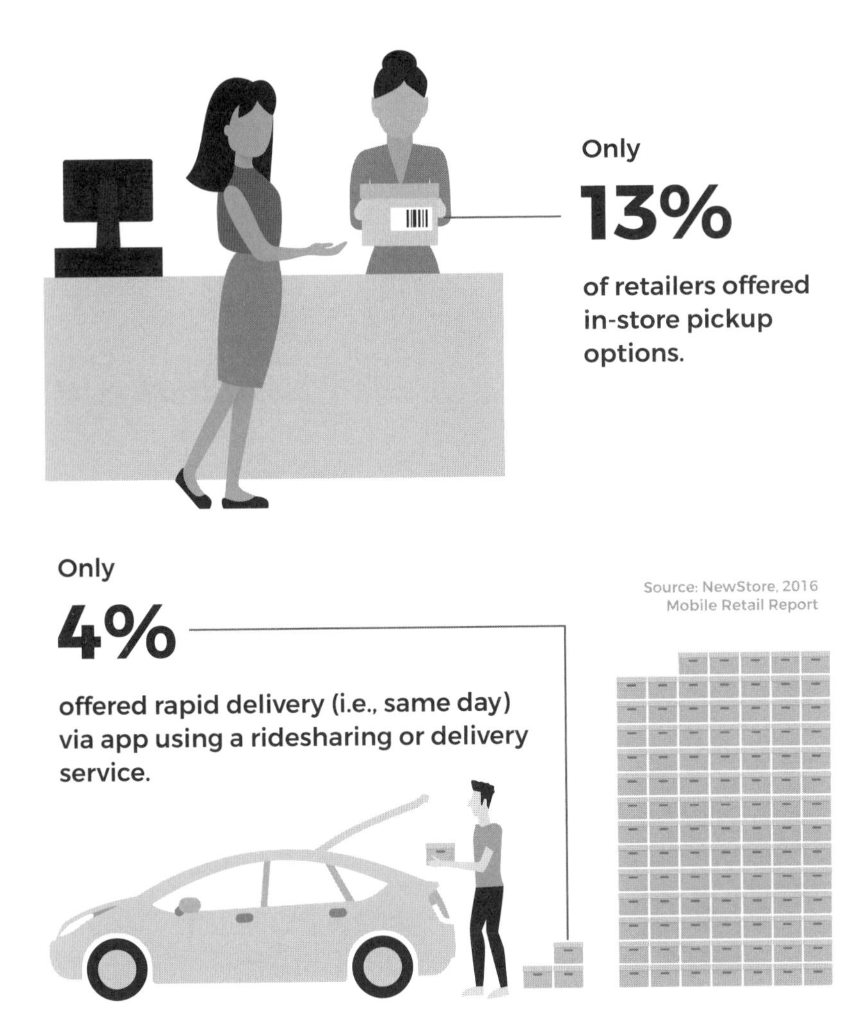


### *To Wrap Up:*

- Fulfillment is the key battleground in the transformation of retail for the mobile age. While Amazon has raised the expectations of consumers when it comes to convenience, retailers who use mobile technology can meet and exceed those expectations.

- Existing disrupters such as ridesharing firms can assist retailers as they shift their fulfillment methods to a mobile-driven process. This will increase as ride-sharing expands and innovations such as driverless cars enter the marketplace. By tapping into existing transportation options, retailers can give consumers the personalized experience they desire.
- Amazon, as successful as it is, is a virtual vending machine concept. Retailers can beat it by using mobile technology to offer what vending machines cannot – a personalized experience.

### *Next Steps:*

- Turn brick-and-mortar stores into your biggest asset.
- Provide same day delivery and returns using your stores as fulfillment centers.
- Offer convenience and a high-touch consumer experience.
- Take advantage of the modern fulfillment methods offered by Deliv, UberRUSH, and similar same day delivery services.
- Train your associates and stockroom workers to use the new service providers.
- Incorporate elements of delight to create a remarkable experience as part of the fulfillment process.

## Voices from the Mobile Makeover

*Rachel Ferguson, Footwear Buyer, Cambridge Select*

If there's a spot in the customer journey that Rachel Ferguson thinks can be improved, it's fulfillment. With all the focus on speed and efficiency, everyone seems to have forgotten about the experience.

"Fulfillment can be a good customer experience. In fact, it used to be," Ferguson says. Working as a team leader for a department store in the early days of ecommerce, it was her job to pick and pack the items ordered via the fledgling online system. "When we started out and there weren't that many orders, we'd put handwritten thank you notes into the packages before we sent them," she recalled. But as the business built, so did the pressure. "At holiday time, it was 'Forget the note; just ship it!'"

Something has been lost in that hurry. With mobile commerce putting a renewed focus on the fulfillment experience, Rachel sees an opportunity to delight customers. "We've gotten used to the bare-bones Amazon delivery," she says, referring to a product stuffed in a brown box or plain envelope with no magic, no whimsy, no thank you. "We're settling," she says. "Fulfillment can be a great customer experience."

*Chapter 9*

# The Brand Relationship Makeover

**Insights**

- Future-proofing a brand for the mobile age will involve every aspect of a company, from technologists to marketers.
- Thanks to user-generated content, customers will be involved in brand management in increasingly important ways.

At the dawn of the new millennium, a new concept made the rounds of marketing circles: 360-degree branding. Legendary advertising executive Shelly Lazarus led her agency Ogilvy & Mather and the entire advertising industry into this extreme new concept. The theory suggested a brand could transcend the confines of a single message and be experienced by customers in an all-encompassing way. It was a leap to think branding could be that present – always on, always around you, always in communication with the customer – but who knew that was only the beginning?

# Steps to Future-Proof Your Brand for the Mobile Age

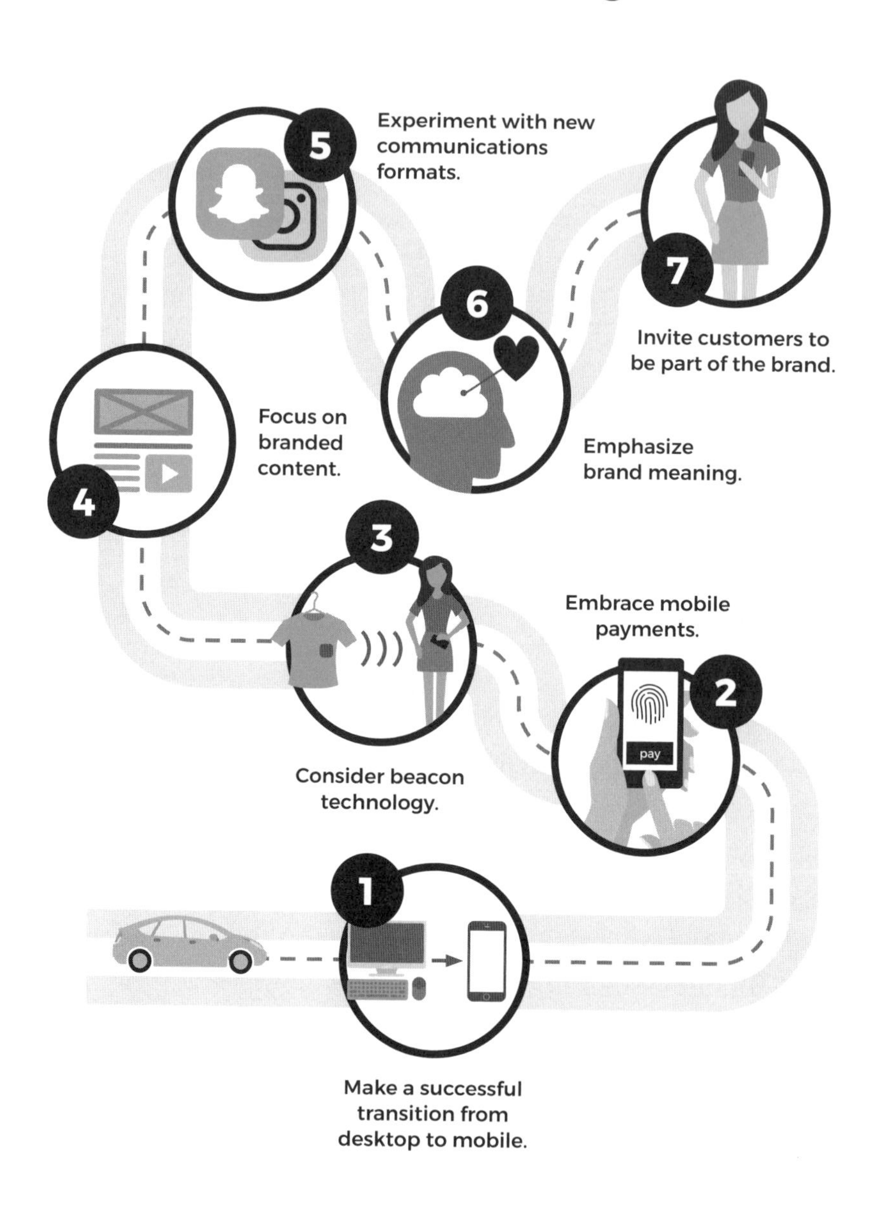

Today, mobile makes the concept of 360-degree marketing seem staid. Forget having the brand all around you; now we meld with our favorite brands, giving and receiving data constantly. We are our brands, and they are us.

The expansion of the brand experience means the expansion of the branding process. Branding is no longer the sole silo of an agency. Creating, nurturing, and sustaining a brand is a task that touches every decision a company makes. Can you future-proof your brand? Yes, but you can't rely on your agency to do all the work. In a brand relationship makeover, the realization that brand is far more than just message is clear. That makes future-proofing the brand for the mobile age everyone's job. Branding needs a makeover, one that recognizes the flip to mobile, and this requires taking several steps.

## *Steps to Future-Proof Your Brand for the Mobile Age*

### Step One: Make a Successful Transition from Desktop to Mobile

Start with the small screen in mind. Mobile is the "everywhere" channel, and consumers choose mobile when other channels – laptops, desktops – are just a few feet away. Brands looking to secure the future will mirror their customers' preference for the small screen. They'll put resources into mobile and plan on mobile interaction being the primary connection to shoppers.

Part of that transition includes the move from websites to apps. Mobile apps win versus mobile browsers because they are designed from the ground up to take advantage of mobile features such as gestures (swiping, pinching, etc.)

and location. Mobile websites are slow because they use a DOM, or document object model. It doesn't make sense to deliver the most critical and stable elements of a customer interface over slow and intermittently unavailable mobile bandwidth. Size matters. Clever retailers will recognize this and design content natively with the small screen in mind. Mobile apps allow better interactivity and personalization. They can perform many of their functions while offline. Mobile apps have GPS capabilities and can send push notifications that can be leveraged, using beacon technology, to give an extraordinary cross-channel experience.

As part of this process, audit your agency talent to be sure your people have made the move to mobile. Look for talent that thinks of the small screen first and can create messaging appropriate to the mobile medium.

### Step Two: Embrace Mobile Payments

Retailers are already spending the money to upgrade their point-of-sale environments to be compliant with the new card association mandates to accept EMV (chip) cards. If you're going to spend the money anyway, look for a solution that's mobile payment friendly (Apple Pay, Android Pay) as well. Mobile payments are actually more secure than their traditional "card swipe" counterparts, so why not embrace mobile payments for consumers' convenience and safety?

Mobile payments can also take place in the store. Cashless checkout means shorter lines, which means happier customers. Equip your sales staff with mobile card readers and have them intercept customers whenever there are more than two in line. Allow customers to make in-store purchases using a native consumer app installed on their mobile devices.

## Step Three: Focus on Branded Content

Forrester Research reports that companies are looking to branded content in order to perform better in search optimization, as well as to boost conversion rates. Consumers, they've found, buy more when they're engaged by good content. One retailer in the study found that relevant content boosted incremental income by 5% per year[28].

The Barneys New York app makes content part of its process. The app opens to branded photographs linking consumers to keep up with what's current, such as the upcoming season's products or the ability to shop what's been seen on the runway at New York Fashion Week. Scroll down a little further, and you'll see the latest fashion stories that have been posted to the app in addition to some of their featured categories.

## Step Four: Emphasize Brand Meaning

As consumers, brands have always been concepts we reach for to complete our identities. We look for tribes to belong to, banners to wave, ideas to embrace. To deliver this to consumers, we can't simply call on a team of engineers. We need to reach out for talent that can utilize emotion and identity. These are the tools that help us understand and shape our world. When we look to advertising agencies today, we should be asking for additional skill sets such as anthropology and psychology. These are the skill sets we can use to build technology platforms as well as the brands that will strike emotional chords and build lasting relationships.

Brand meaning is the driver of many a consumer decision. First-world consumers rarely make decisions based on actual need. We live in a world in which production and consumption are part of our daily lives, and what we buy is often not so much what we need but what we want. We don't buy Dr. Pepper because we're thirsty; we buy it because "I'm a Pepper!" We drive a Prius not because we need it to get to work but because we want to think of ourselves as people who care about the environment. Our consumption has meaning to us. The brand creates that meaning.

Agencies have always been our partners in creating and communicating meaning. If your agency is all about technical specs and isn't talking to you about consumer culture theory and its study of consumption choices and behaviors, you might be missing a critical skill set in your branding for the mobile age.

### Step Five: Experiment with New Communication Formats

Retailers have been slow to adopt new ways of using digital technology to communicate with customers. Our *Mobile Retail Report* found that only 27% of brands sent personalized communication after an online purchase. To stay relevant, retailers must do that and more. Fashion icons Marc Jacobs and Alexander Wang took a risk when they ventured onto Snapchat to promote their brands. This is new territory for high fashion, given that full control of the brand image is often paramount. How can the fleeting nature of Snapchat fit into that carefully crafted process? By using Snapchat to invite customers to an exclusive event or capture a moment at Fashion Week, the fashion brands showed that they too can grow and evolve with technology, just as their customers have. This process of co-creation, where a brand uses but does not fully control the platform, offers great rewards but also risk. These firms aren't designed to experiment and flex with new opportunities. In fact, they have long functioned in a far more controlled environment, so their willingness to experiment and cede some control is a great leap.

Experimenting with new communication formats might also require an understanding of new elements that are both risky and beneficial, such as user-generated content. We've all seen that consumers are most impressed with the reviews of actual purchasers. We've all been there, reading the comments section before making a purchase or glancing through the reviews before making a reservation. We care what our fellow customers have to say, and we even give that raw commentary status.

For some, the first step might come by reaching consumers via the apps they already use most: Facebook, Instagram, Whatsapp, and Snapchat. Facebook in particular is looking to integrate shopping into its experience. For brands, this presents an opportunity to connect.

### Step Six: Invite Customers to Be Part of the Brand

Create experiences that give customers a chance to be part of the brand. GoPro encourages users of the camera to post their action videos for everyone to view. Some brands reward customers for posting selfies or photos of themselves wearing the products. Some companies designate "brand ambassadors" and ask them to blog about new products and to wear them at parties. Lululemon offers yoga classes in its stores. All these programs invite customers to immerse themselves in the brand and be part of it.

Ultimately, future-proofing your brand means making sure your company adapts to the ways consumers want to interact with your brand. The consequences of not future-proofing can be dire – look at how once famous, once dominant brands like Borders, Blockbuster, FAO Schwarz, and Washington Mutual Bank have all collectively declined and ended up in the dead pool. Avoiding that fate is everybody's job.

## *To Wrap Up:*

- Protecting your brand in a mobile world means much more than advertising and marketing. To future-proof your brand, make changes throughout the company from technology choices to store associate policies. In the mobile age, brand management is not a siloed activity; your brand is impacted by every action your company takes.

- Content is king. Deeper, richer, more experiential content will drive your brand. Content can be product focused or activity focused, but all content is an interaction with your customer and an opportunity to create and future-proof a brand.

- Be willing to experiment with new tactics. Future-proofing your brand might involve everything from trying beacon technology in your stores to experimenting with Instagram.

## *Next Steps:*

- Assess your current brand talent. Does your team have the skills to help you create brand meaning? Do you have both engineers and anthropologists on the project? Can you expand future-proofing efforts to involve more than just the agency or the marketing department?
- Share ownership. Who owns the brand? Don't be afraid to give it multiple owners, since that only reflects the reality of the marketplace. Brands that cling to the idea of a one-man band in brand management are living in a bygone era. That level of control, while once successful, is no longer possible. Accept the mobile transformation of brand ownership and reconfigure your efforts to manage and reflect that wider brand family.
- Recognize the time squeeze. When message and delivery take place on the same small screen, your time to deliver brand messaging has been dramatically reduced, possibly to seconds. Understand how physical technology has changed the process of brand marketing. Learn to work without the benefit of the old equation. You no longer have the luxury of that time.

## Voices from the Mobile Makeover

*Dawn Trenson, Director, Ecommerce Operations, Intermix*

How do you future-proof your brand?

With a little courage and a lot of variety.

Dawn Trenson says the constant change in retail-related technology is both a gift and a curse. She explains, "The ever-changing mobile landscape is a 'gift' because there seems to be a monthly 'next big thing'/new outlet for us to connect with our customers to (hopefully) connect content with commerce. Best illustration of this: Instagram and the blogging industry that was subsequently born. Having the 'right' Instagram influencer touting your brand is often more valuable than a coveted spot in a September issue of a fashion magazine." She continues, "[The ever-changing mobile landscape is] a 'curse' as continual evolution equates to continual investment in technology to power marketing efforts. It can be challenging to justify continuing expenditures."

But doing so makes sense, especially since millennial shoppers never knew life before the internet and never go shopping without their smartphones. "Brands and retailers need to not only adopt but also embrace mobile technology across all customer touch points [in order to stay relevant]," Trenson says. She concludes, "Mobile technology on the front line — from brick-and-mortar stores to wholesale showrooms to front row at New York Fashion Week — needs to be welcomed as the conduit for all branded experiences."

*Epilogue:*

# Mobile Up

## *Where do we go from here?*

One more makeover needs to happen. It happens not in our stores and not on our screens but in the way we think about retail. It requires a fundamental rethinking of how brands are built with a focus on more intense customer relationships. I call this makeover: mobile up.

Mobile first is a concept that's been in the business discussion space for several years. It's the idea that websites should be built first for mobile and then for desktop and other platforms. This was the early call to direct resources toward mobile, but it doesn't go far enough because mobile first only targets websites and other front-end experiences.

Mobile up, on the other hand, reflects a deeper and more significant shift in the retail process. Instead of simply moving resources around, a mobile up process demands a completely new starting point. Activity shifts from optimizing digital experiences for mobile to creating entirely new businesses from mobile on up.

A mobile up business is one in which the customer has a remote control for her favorite brand in the palm of her hand. This humanization of brands allows one-on-one interactions between customers and companies. This is a true evolution in the customer experience. Mass emails and advertising campaigns have always spoken broadly *at* customers, not *with* them. To be sure, tailored product recommendations were offered based on past purchases and browsing, but those ultimately lacked intimacy. Now, mobile provides the opportunity to reshape the interaction between brands and customers. Frankly, we're just starting to uncover the possibilities.

If websites allowed brands to build communities, mobile empowers brands to be built for individuals, in the most positive context of that word. Mobile up leads to a two-way conversation between brands and customers, creating a relationship that is deep and dynamic. Mobile is the first medium that allows both parties to intimately connect with each other while sharing the brands' values, language, and aesthetics.

Until recently, mobile has mainly been used as a tool to augment existing experiences, but the focus is shifting. The future is building not just front-end experiences but entire businesses. Don't think mobile first. Think mobile up.

# Endnotes

1. "Mobile Retail Report," NewStore, 2016.
2. "U.S. Retail Mcommerce Sales," 2014–2020, eMarketer, Feb. 2016.
3. "The New Digital Divide," Deloitte, 2016.
4. "How to Win at Customer Service: Keep It Simple," eMarketer, October 15, 2015.
5. "Winning in the Age of the Customer," Forrester Research, Inc., April 6, 2015.
6. "The Transformation of the Store," Ken Morris, CIO Review, December 7, 2015.
7. "Shoppers Want More from in-Store Mobile," DMI, 2015.
8. "The Store Associate Dilemma: Mobile Enablement, So Close Yet So Far," NewStore.
9. "The State of Retail 2015 Report," TimeTrade.
10. "The Store Associate Dilemma: Mobile Enablement, So Close Yet So Far," NewStore.
11. "Master Your Mobile Loyalty Moment," Forrester Research, Inc., April 26, 2016.
12. "Walmart Introduces Walmart Pay," news.walmart.com, December 10, 2015.

13. "How Retailers Like Michael Kors Are Turning Instagram into Customer Loyalty Vehicles," Hilary Milnes, *Glossy*, July 25, 2016.

14. "Leadership in the Age of the Customer," Forrester Research, Inc., April 26, 2016.

15. "The State of Loyalty Strategies 2016," Forrester Research, Inc., April 7, 2016.

16. "Leadership in the Age of the Customer," Forrester Research, Inc., April 26, 2016.

17. "Why Your Mobile App Could Fail," Ryan Darby and Sean Williams, Gallup, April 29, 2014.

18. "4 Ways Retailers Increase Sales with Mobile-Enabled Foot Traffic Analytics," David Strom, Softwareadvice.com, February 13, 2014.

19. "Analyze This: Web Style Analytics Enters the Retail Store," Forrester Research, Inc., March 30, 2016.

20. "Customer Engagement: Data Capture," L2 Inc., May 1, 2015.

21. "The Uber-ization of Retail," Stephan Schambach, *Internet Retailer*, January 12, 2016.

22. "Retail Innovations: Omnichannel," L2 Inc., Insight Report.

23. "Future-proofing Your Brand: Leveraging Shipping as a Competitive Advantage," NewStore.

24. "Don't Get Left at the Starting Gate: Learn How to Meet Fulfillment Expectations," NewStore.

25. L2 Inc., "Curbside Offers Better Fulfillment with In-Store Pickup."

26. *Internet Retailer*, August 30, 2016.

27. "Online Retailers Tackle High Rate of Customer Returns," Susanna Kim, abcnews.com, December 24, 2013.

28. "Making Content Work for Retail," Forrester Research, Inc., January 27, 2016.

# Acknowledgments

This book came together thanks to the expertise and generosity of many people in my professional circle.

Thanks to Scott Galloway for his continued support and wisdom and for agreeing to write the foreword of this book.

Thanks to the many industry professionals who shared their time and insights to help bring the information in this book to life: Dino Becirovic of KPCB, Tim Bridge of minubo, Martijn Cornelissen of Rituals, Richard Last of Axcelora, Harm Ohlmeyer of adidas, Ted McNamara of M.Gemi, Scott Lux of John Varvatos, Robert Gentz of Zalando, Dawn Trenson of Intermix, Daren Hull of Outdoor Voices, and Rachel Ferguson of Cambridge Select. Your voices from the front lines of mobile transformation enhance and enliven these pages.

Thank you to the team at Jenkins Group for their professionalism and patience as this book moved from idea to reality: Jerrold Jenkins, Leah Nicholson, Yvonne Fetig Roehler, Jim Kalajian, and Ellen Neuborne.

Thank you to Daniel Brylla, who tirelessly worked on the graphics for this book.

Finally, thank you to the many members of the NewStore team who brought their keen understanding of mobile transformation to the project. Thank you to Ana Milevskaja, who championed this book through its many stages, and also to the NewStore teammates who stepped up and contributed to the cause: Casey Antonelli, Margie Bell, Tony DiPaolo, Phil Granof, Kai-Thomas Krause, Ulrike Mueller, Ann Pham, Alexander Ringsdorff, Kristin Schepici, and Richie Siegel.

# About the Author

Stephan Schambach is a serial entrepreneur who brought us ecommerce and has shaken up the industry on multiple occasions. He was a pioneer in creating the first standard software for online shopping in 1995. In addition to founding Intershop Communications, he also founded Demandware and NewStore.

Schambach grew up in East Germany, where he graduated from Polytechnic High School. After the fall of the Berlin Wall and the following monetary union, Schambach left his apprenticeship as a laboratory technician in physics and became a partner in the Hard & Soft Stanja KG in Jena. In 1992, he founded the NetConsult Computer Systeme GmbH. After the first in-house development called Archive 2000, the company presented the ecommerce software Intershop Online.

NetConsult secured venture capital funding to guarantee further development and active international marketing measures. Further financial rounds enabled robust growth for more than a few hundred employees worldwide.

In 1996, Schambach established the first U.S. location for the company in Burlingame, California, near San Francisco. Prior to its IPO, Intershop software naming rights were acquired from the Swiss Intershop AG. Meanwhile, the company was renamed Intershop Communications. The IPO took place on the Neuer Markt in 1998 and on the U.S. NASDAQ stock exchange in 2000. Schambach ceded his position as chairman of the board in 2003.

In 2004, he founded the U.S. company Demandware, Inc., and offered the first ecommerce solution as a cloud service. Demandware was listed on the New York Stock Exchange (NYSE) in 2012 and was acquired by Salesforce in 2016 for $2.8 billion.

In 2015, Schambach founded NewStore, Inc., and led efforts to create the first Mobile Retail Platform. Schambach is also involved as an investor and board member at various ecommerce startups and serves as chairman in the electro mobility business with Torqeedo.

In addition to his work as an entrepreneur, Schambach has committed himself to improving the environment for start-ups and high-growth companies in Germany. This includes improving the practices of funding and exit opportunities. Further, he and the Intershop Foundation are major sponsors of the ecommerce chair at the University of Applied Sciences in Jena, Germany.

For his contribution to developing the software industry in Thuringia, Germany, he received the National Order of Merit in 2000.